A Charmed Life

by
Peter Juge

Bloomington, IN  Milton Keynes, UK

authorHOUSE®

AuthorHouse™
1663 Liberty Drive, Suite 200
Bloomington, IN 47403
www.authorhouse.com
Phone: 1-800-839-8640

AuthorHouse™ UK Ltd.
500 Avebury Boulevard
Central Milton Keynes, MK9 2BE
www.authorhouse.co.uk
Phone: 08001974150

This book is a work of non-fiction. Unless otherwise noted, the author and the publisher make no explicit guarantees as to the accuracy of the information contained in this book and in some cases, names of people and places have been altered to protect their privacy.

First published by AuthorHouse 12/13/2006

ISBN: 978-1-4259-8153-2 (sc)

Printed in the United States of America
Bloomington, Indiana

This book is printed on acid-free paper.

Library of Congress Control Number: 2006910488

Dedication

To my wife, Nancy, who provided the real charm in my life. To my kids, Suzy and David, who have always made me proud to be their father. To their mates, Greg and Anne, troopers both. And to my grandchildren, Kate, Jack and Lindsay who should all be wearing haloes.

Other books by Peter Juge:

Non-Fiction:

    Come Taste the Wine

    Matey's Tour de France

Fiction:

    Agent Matey to the Rescue

    Agent Matey's Assignment in Brittany

    Agent Matey at the Feet of the Ancients

Poetry:

    Matey's Petite Collection

Autobiography:

    A Charmed Life

The cover painting is by the 19th century Japanese artist Hokusai. It is *Sumi* and color on paper depicting an *oni* cowering under a hat during a Settsubun Festival; signed *Gakuro jin Manji hitsu* with a red Fuji seal; in the collection of the author who acquired it from Sotheby's in 1980.

Contents

Peter at Age 8
(after a romp in a muddy churchyard)

Chapter 1. The Interview

Early on in my retirement, a psychiatrist who was treating me for long standing bipolar disorder pinned me down about how much I drank. When I told him, he exclaimed "Wow! Do you realize how much alcohol that is?"

I pointed out to him I had been drinking like that my entire adult life. He looked at my last blood work results and remarked,

"I can't believe it; your liver function test is normal."

"That's the way it's always been," I told him.

"Look, this bothers me; it's pertinent to your condition. I want you to do something for me."

"Sure what to you want me to do?"

"I want you to see a psychologist on our staff. She is an expert on the subject."

"What subject?"

"Alcohol."

"Sure; I look forward to meeting her."

So we met. You know essentially what happens in these sessions is you are paying somebody to listen to you talk.

Dr. Jones told me, "Dr. Smith is concerned about the amount you drink every day." Then she went over how much the psychiatrist told her I drank.

She wasn't asking a question so I just kept quiet.

"Tell me about yourself."

"You want to know about everything or just about the liquor?"

"Just the liquor for now."

"OK here we go."

"I grew up in New Orleans where the culture was Mediterranean and there were no rules. My parents had drinks every evening. Sometimes they let me have a sip. It was part of my education they said."

"My grandfather was a first generation American. His father had come to Louisiana from France as a young boy. We always had wine at his table, even the grandchildren. He would pour our glasses, wine cut with water. As we grew older our wine grew redder."

"Then there was high school. From freshman on up to senior we drank beer. How much depended on how much money we made at part-time jobs. As long as you could get the money up on the counter, you could buy beer. I'm not sure about booze; I never tried. Beer was what we drank in high school.

"Did you ever get drunk?" the psychologist asked.

"We sure did. That's what it was all about then. It was only later that we learned to pace ourselves."

"Hmm."

"So to continue, in college we graduated to booze, mostly bourbon, it was the South after all. That was the first time I experienced 'hangovers' terrible things. I was in a fraternity at Tulane University. At parties at the fraternity house people passed out all the time. One evening we stretched out a fraternity brother, who had passed out across the threshold of the front door. He was a popular guy whom girls stooped to pat or kiss on the cheek as they entered the house for the party. The Dean of Men appeared, paying a call as he sometimes did. He stepped over our comatose brother and remarked as he entered the house 'glad you boys didn't let Bob fall and hurt himself;' then the Dean made his way to the bar to get a drink."

"I was only a year at Tulane. My grades were pitiful. This was not surprising for a guy who majored in poker and bourree'(a Louisiana card game). I really blew it. I washed out of the Navy ROTC program. The Korean War had broken out the previous summer and being dismissed from the Navy program put me at the head of the line to be drafted. I didn't want to go to Korea and live in a foxhole. I wanted to be on a ship. So I enlisted in the Coast Guard. The service committment was three years as compared to four in the Navy."

"Say Dr. Jones am I going into too much detail?"

"Oh no you're doing just fine."

So I then told her about the Coast Guard. "I was a sailor, a white hat; and what do they do ashore? They drink. We didn't have a lot of money so it was mostly beer. But in one Port moonshine was available at $5 a gallon."

"So it went for three years, but I grew up a bit."

"When I finished my three-year hitch, I enrolled at LSU. I couldn't afford the tuition at Tulane."

"LSU turned out to be just right for me. I could make it on the GI-Bill. It was away from New Orleans and my old haunts. I did resume my fraternity activities but I had learned to pace myself. After three years at LSU, I graduated Phi Beta Kappa and passed the US Foreign Service exam."

"So I became a diplomat and served at American Embassies in Ethiopia, Malaysia and Cameroon. What do diplomats do? They drink. Sometimes there are two or more cocktail parties an evening. I married my childhood sweetheart Nancy who then followed me around the world and raised our kids. She was quite a lady; and she could drink me under the table anytime."

"Then Mobil Oil came along and offered me money to become its government relations advisor in Nigeria. The company was starting up an offshore producing play during the Biafran War. So I became an international oilman, and after Nigeria I served in two more Mobil start-up operations in Indonesia and Saudi Arabia. In Saudi Arabia where alcoholic beverages are banned I made red wine from grape juice sugar and baking yeast. It was not bad. Following my foreign assignments Mobil sent me to Mobil's headquarters in Manhattan, and then to Mobil's labs in Princeton. They made me a Vice President. Manhattan was the land of the three martini lunch, and in the evenings I rode the New Haven commuter train to Westport. I seldom failed to meet my friends in the bar car."

"I retired from Mobil in 1989 when I was 57 years-old. That's pretty much it".

"That is an amazing story; since you retired what are you doing?"

"I told her about my volunteer activities and writing.

"What about the death of your wife? Has this affected your drinking at all?"

"I don't think so. She and I both had our daily activities after I retired. We got together at cocktail time to chat and compare notes. We were drinking buddies. I miss her. I never remarried because I never found anyone who measured up to her. Drinking alone is not as much fun as with somebody. But I don't think it's had any effect on my drinking habits."

"Look, you've had an admirable career, but was there ever any time that your drinking affected your work? Did you get tipsy at parties sometimes and offend someone you had to apologize to later? Did you ever miss work?"

"No, my wife was very good at nudging me at parties when it was time to leave. My upbringing taught me never to offend anyone unintentionally. I never ever missed work. Mobil's work day starts early around the world. At headquarters this meant getting up at 4:30 and catching a 5:30 train, so I could be at my desk by seven. I nefver missed the 5:30 train.

"Since your retirement have there been any alcohol associated incidents that affected your life?"

"Well I did break my neck."

"You did what?"

"I fell from a loft in my cabin in West Virginia and broke my neck. The doctors had to perform an operation to fuse three cervical vertebrae."

"Good God Peter! How did this happen?" -

"Well it was the 4th of July weekend. My daughter, Suzy and our two grandchildren, Kate and Jack were spending the weekend with us at the cabin. The grand kids were asleep in the loft. Suzy would join them later. Before dinner, Nancy made me a couple of her famous gargantuan martinis. Then, we had wine with the splendid dinner my wife and daughter had cooked."

"There was no john in the loft, and Suzy reminded me after dinner to take the portapotty up there. She wanted to avoid having to carry the kids down the circular staircase during the night to the bathroom on the ground floor. So I picked up the portapotty which had been cleaned and recharged with the blue stuff, and headed up the circular staircase."

"The portapotty was not light and when I reached the top of the stairs, I was huffing and puffing. What greeted me there? A closed kiddy gate, Suzy had installed to assure no kids would awake and fall down the circular staircase. I had two options; I could back down the staircase with the portapotty or I could step over the gate. The portapotty was getting heavier by the minute, so I decided on the latter option. My right foot made it over OK, but my left foot didn't. I began to fall right on top of Jack who was in his sleeping bag just below me. I managed somehow to make a spin to the left so I'd miss Jack. But my spin sent me crashing through the loft railing along with the portapotty to the floor below. I regained consciousness looking up at Nancy and Suzy hovering over me. I was unable to move. The infernal portapotty lay across the room unscathed."

"The cabin was in a remote valley in West Virginia, and we had no telephone then. Nancy drove off into the misty dark night to find a rescue squad. They took me to a hospital in Virginia. In the emergency room, I lay on a bed next to a boy about Jack's age who had been bitten by a copperhead. Who was worse off, I thought. As it turned out I was – an operation on my spinal column followed by months of recuperation wearing a neck brace. The snake-bit kid walked out of the hospital the next morning"

The psychologist turned to me and said "Now Mr. Juge wasn't that a message for you that alcohol nearly cost you your life?"

"Not at all. It saved my life! The doctor told me if I hadn't had those martinis to relax me, the fall would probably have killed me."

"Mr. Juge. You are a very exasperating person, engaging but still exasperating. All I can say to you is, you lead a charmed life."

Chapter 2. New Orleans

Growing up in New Orleans was great. Most of my memories are good ones. I was born during the depression. At that time my father didn't have a job and we lived with my grandparents. I was the first grandchild. My great grandmother was alive at the time and I am told she taught me songs in French and German.

Also I am told I was a precocious child but a devil. My parents and grandparents were stunned when I started school that I was not a stellar pupil. The teacher told my mother, I was difficult to control. It was that way all the way through grammar school. My mother tired of hearing the teachers' complaints so she stopped going for the conferences and stopped giving me a hard time about my report cards. I was on my own

In those days kids were allowed to roam the neighborhood at will. I ranged two or three blocks in one direction and four-or-so in the other. Evenings we played kick-the-can on the street corners. We played sand lot base ball and touch football. Parents didn't organize kids' sports back then. I had a paper route, and I was a boy scout. I loved being a scout. It was just the right mix of some discipline and lots of slack, and what we did was fun.

My father was the superintendent of the electrical department at Higgins Boat Company with some 800 people working for him at the height of WWII. He worked very long hours during the war and my younger brother and I didn't see that much of him. My brother was four years younger, so we didn't do a lot together. When my father had the time, he hunted deer and ducks. I went with him. I shot my first deer when I was fifteen. Although a stern man he was fun to be with when he was relaxed. The men who worked for him were terrified of him. Once I was sitting outside his office when he was running a meeting. I heard him raking some of his people over the coals. It was frightening to hear. I was sure glad I wasn't the object of his wrath.

My mother was intellectual. She read and played bridge. She was of German protestant descent; my father of French/German Catholic descent. I often wondered how they ever got together.

Religion was a big deal in New Orleans then. My mother raised my brother and me as Episcopalians, much to the chagrin of my father's mother.

My grandfather was well to do. He owned a liquid cargo surveying firm in the Port of New Orleans. His father was French and his mother German. This was not unusual in the bayou country of Louisiana at that time. Culturally, he was a Frenchman. My grandmother was of Alsatian descent. She was an incredibly good cook. I used to spend time with her in her kitchen. She taught me a lot. I remember several pots bubbling on the stove with bones sticking out of them. "Beef, chicken and veal stock" she told me; "the secret of good food."

My mother's father was from an old, well-to-do, New Orleans family. He was offered the opportunity to go to college as his siblings did but he chose business. He owned one of the first automobile tire businesses in New Orleans. His partner turned out to be a charlatan and wheeler-dealer. In time, the business failed. My grandfather ended up supporting his family quite well from winnings he garnered playing whist in several of the gentlemen's clubs in the city. His older brother was a prominent lawyer. His sister was an opera singer who married a French Count.

My grandmother's father was a banker. His first wife died when he was in his forties and he took a girl of 18 as his second wife. She and my grandmother were the same age. The two girls became very thick. They used to play tricks on my great-grandfather. To preserve his dignity he enrolled my grandmother in the St. Louis Conservatory of Music to get her out of town. She was my favorite relative. She had a great sense of humor and was warm and fun to be with. She lived with us toward the end of her life.

I attended Lusher Grammar School just a block from my house. I was not much of a student. Nothing really interested me. In the sixth grade they gave us IQ tests. One of my least favorite teachers, Miss D told me I was average. She admonished me that if I paid more attention in class, my score might improve.

Miss D and I just could not get along. She didn't really know the subject matter. My mother taught me more grammar than she did. She was disorganized. Sometimes she didn't know where she was in the syllabus. I couldn't resist saying irreverent things soto voce about her that broke up my class mates. She often sent me out of class to the Principal's office to be disciplined. I got along well with the Principal. She gave me books from her personal library to read while I did time in her waiting room. I remember reading Voltaire's *Candide*. The Principal and I discussed it when I finished. I remember thinking "now that's interesting."

One day this same teacher kept me after school, and sent me to the library to cool my heels. I found a book or two to glance through and the time passed. Later I was looking out the window when I saw the teacher getting into her car and driving off. She had forgotten about me. "Wow" I thought, "What am I going to do with this?"

The scheme came to me fairly quickly. I went home. The next morning I put on the same clothes I'd worn the day before. I got to school early and headed for the library.

I saw her when she arrived. She always parked in the same place. I heard her go into her classroom. I heard her footsteps as she headed to library. I heard her grunt of surprise when she found the door unlocked. I put my head down on a library table. She came in the library. She saw me. She remembered. She screamed.

I might have gotten off lighter if I hadn't laughed. She almost hit me. She certainly wanted to. She sent me straight to the Principal's office. The Principal gave me a look when I came into her waiting room so early in the day. She went into her office and closed the door. She came out shortly, barely suppressing a smile. "That was a naughty trick you played on Miss D. OK let's continue your liberal education." She winked. I winked back. She handed me two books. I remember one of them was *The Last of the Mohicans.* "I'm going to give you a quiz on these."

After about three days or so, I was told to return to Miss D's classroom. I tried to get along with her, and she tried to get along with me. It worked. I made it through the rest of the term. Miss D. gave me an "S" – satisfactory, the lowest passing grade. She no doubt wanted me to move on. I'm sure the Principal had something to do with this as well. And so I graduated from Lusher Grammar School.

High school was much better. At grammar school, a class was 15 kids tops. At Alcee Fortier High School there were close to a hundred in the freshmen class. I wasn't the only cut-up. There were several, but I have to say none was as imaginative as I.

By and large the teachers were better. I liked English, Geometry, and Physics, also Music. My grades were weak. I found I could get by without studying by paying attention in class. I received very few A's but no D's and no F's.

I liked Music because the teacher was young and good looking. She taught us to sing all the songs that were popular then. I'll always remember one two-hundred pound football player in our class putting his heart into "Tea for Two." She also had a knack for keeping the students under control. We respected her.

I had jobs during the summer and part-time jobs during the school year. I worked for my grandfather's firm sometimes. This was how I funded my main activities, dating and partying. Drive-in movies were big then also restaurants with car-hops. Occasionally when I was flush, we'd go down to the French Quarter and listen to Jazz. A 7 ounce beer cost a dollar and you could nurse it for an hour or so. The waiters didn't bother us. My father was generous in letting me use his car in the evenings. It was a 1940 Ford he had nursed through the war years.

Fortier was considered the best public high school in New Orleans. There was a Catholic high school run by Jesuits and several private schools. Some of my classmates from Lusher went to one or the other of those, though most went to Fortier. We all met again at Tulane or LSU. I don't recall knowing anyone who went away to college.

In those days, we were separated by gender in high school as well as by race. Fortier was an all-boy's institution. McMain, the girl's school, was three blocks away. There was a path worn between Fortier and McMain Not that we could get in, but we could chat with the girls through the fence during PE when there wasn't a teacher on guard. The girls wore bloomers in PE then.

In my senior year I was elected Fortier's "Ideal Boyfriend" by the faculty. Strange for an all-boy's institution but there was a competition with all the other high schools in the city and I was Fortier's entry. All I got out of this was a lot of ribbing from my friends. The girls at McMain didn't take any particular notice of my new title.

I was not a jock. I tried out for track, but didn't make the cut. I played a role in the senior class play that was a co-ed production with the girls from McMain.

I learned in grammar school, if I was going to do anything unruly, it was preferable to do it as part of a group. I liked being the conceiver and organizer in such activity. There was one teacher absolutely no one liked. He could not control his class – not an easy task in an all-boy's school sure – but he was mean and vindictive. We got together to discuss what to do. They liked my plan. Several of the guys lifted his small car and put it inside the railings that protected the lawns on the side of the school. He had to order a tow truck to get his car out. But that was not all. We had removed his hub caps, put a hand full of raw shrimp in the wheels, and pushed the hub caps back on. He never could figure out where the stink was coming from. He eventually had to get rid of the car.

I graduated from Fortier in 1950 with a C average. I have no idea where I ranked in my class, somewhere near the bottom probably. However I passed the Navy ROTC exam which provided a full scholarship to any of a number of fine colleges – Harvard, Yale, Princeton, etc. etc. I had no desire to leave New Orleans; I applied to Tulane and was accepted. Passing this exam was seminal for me. I was one of only two of a number of my classmates to pass it. It was the first time I realized I had some brains.

Chapter 3. Tulane

I was at Tulane only a year, but WOW! what a year it was. My Navy ROTC scholarship paid tuition and books, plus I received fifty dollars a month pocket money. This was in 1950. I was 18 years old trim and handsome. I had a car, a WWII vintage Willys Jeep that I bought from summer earnings. I mounted a pair of deer antlers as the hood ornament, and attached a confederate flag facing aft. I thought I owned the world.

I made scant use of the brains I discovered I had passing the Navy exam. At Fortier I never studied. I listened in class, did my written homework, and got C's. I thought I would be able to get by doing the same at Tulane. What a rude awakening.

The Kappa Alpha Order made me a bid and I joined. My generous grandfather would give me a ten dollar bill from time-to-time when I visited him. Fraternity brothers would put a dollar's worth of gas in when they borrowed my jeep; I was rolling in money.

This was in the days before computers. To register for classes at Tulane then, one filled out what was called a "train-ticket," a perforated form that was about a couple of yards long. There were sections for each class, and for the various administrative offices of the university. You had to write your name address and all that stuff about 25 times. I had decided I was going to major in journalism mainly because I knew and admired a columnist for the Times Picayune.

I arranged my schedule so I had the afternoons off and no Saturday classes. I took the usual stuff for freshmen, mostly required subjects – English, History, Algebra, Physics and French.

Just across the street from the KA house was Top's Tea Room a student hang-out café where one could play poker, bourree' and bridge for money. An upperclassman fraternity brother (who incidentally went on to become a Jesuit Priest after graduation) borrowed five bucks from me one day shortly after classes began. He promised to pay me back, plus half of whatever he won. Later that afternoon he handed me five dollars and five more. WOW! I thought, that's the thing for me. .

I had a steady girlfriend who was a junior in high school, a good looking blonde. I'd known her since Lusher. I ended up marrying her several years later. Attending fraternity parties with Nancy and playing cards were my principal college activities; those and showing up for most of my classes.

But I must tell you about a memorable incident during my year at Tulane, that had nothing to do with school, KA, or cards. It had to do with a woman. She was definitely a woman, not a girl. She was a good looking, petite blonde with a husky voice. She had her own car, a 1947 Ford coupe. For some reason I didn't understand, she flirted with me. I was a freshman; she was a senior. Wow! I thought, "Maybe it's no more virginity for me!"

Fraternity brothers warned me. "She's strange" they said. "She has this thing about good looking blond freshmen. She's been through several of the brothers. Be careful," they said. "Sure they lost their virginity, but she made them take her to expensive restaurants in the French Quarter and buy her gifts. Then she dumped them. It must have been a brutal experience. Some of them are still getting over it."

"Hey" I thought. "I can handle this." So one evening she drove up to the frat house at a time we had agreed upon. Pointing to the door of her coupe, she said, "Get in." "No," I said, gesturing to my jeep, "You get in." I'd decided it was going to be my way, or not at all. "No wuking fay," she replied, gave me the finger, and burned rubber down the street as she left. I remained a virgin.

Classes were semi interesting. I liked English best; the professor was great. It was my only B at the end of the first semester. The other grades were: a C in Physics, a D in History, the same in Algebra and an F in French. Discovering there was no way I could escape studying even for a D, I dropped French shortly after classes began. I didn't follow the correct procedure for dropping, so this netted me an "incomplete" that later converted to the F. This was the rule. My only out was to take and pass the exam covering the entire semester; fat chance.

The main blow these grades meant for me was I couldn't be initiated into KA; I remained a pledge. Normally the Navy could have cared less what my grades were as long as I didn't flunk out of Tulane, earned my BA in four years and was able to take up my commission. But things had changed since the Korean War had broken out the previous summer. Now they cared.

Commander Eddrington, the Executive Officer, called me in for an interview. "Shape Up!" was his advice. "Have an overall C average by the end of the next semester or you are out of the NROTC program and draft bait!" Agh!

This got my attention, sort of. I put on a little more effort in History and Algebra, and by the end of the semester, I thought I had a lock on the overall C. My plan almost worked.

I got a B in English, a C in History, and a C in Algebra. I got a C in Physics. I was counting on a B. With my pitiful grades from the previous semester I was just short of the overall C. The Navy booted me as promised.

"Oh well" I thought "I'll go to LSU." There was no way I could have afforded staying at Tulane. I knew I could make it at LSU, a state school with low tuition, but "best laid plans," within two weeks of washing out of the NROTC, an order came from my draft board to report for a physical exam and subsequent induction into the United States Army. Woe was me.

Buddies from Fortier had gone to Korea in the Army and Marine reserves. What I heard from them convinced me I didn't want to be a soldier in a foxhole in Korea. I wanted to be a sailor, wherever.

I moved fast. Before the Army could nab me I enlisted for a three-year hitch in the US Coast Guard. I wanted the Navy but they were looking for a 4-year hitch.

Three years as a "white hat" started me on my way to growing up some.

Chapter 4. The Coast Guard

I loved and hated the Coast Guard at the same time. I loved the adventure of going to sea, and hated the boredom of being in port.

I went to boot camp in California. Afterwards, since I was company commander of my boot camp class, I got to choose my assignment. I chose the 8th Coast Guard District in New Orleans. I was assigned to the public relations group, three guys including me.

I had some interesting PR stuff to do, but my principal responsibility was running bets to the Fair Grounds race track. The number two guy in PR was a bookie. He bundled up the bets, along with a sheet specifying which bets went on which horses, in which races. My job was to hop on the street car to the track, lay the bets, collect the winnings and bring it all back. You can see how much work PR had. I didn't play the horses myself; cards were my game.

Fortunately, this didn't last too long. I was assigned to a DE (Destroyer Escort) just being de-mothballed in Florida. The USCG Cutter Durant was scheduled to go on ice berg patrol after outfitting. We made our way from Florida up the east coast stopping in at the Navy weapons depot in Yorktown, Virginia. There we loaded aboard all sorts of munitions and went out to sea and tried them out.

What a day! The depth charges were awesome. It felt like we were being blown out of the water. I was a loader on a 3 inch gun. My job was to push the shell into the breach, then step back and turn to the right. My ears were ringing the whole time. We wore no ear protection back then, and anyone who put cotton in their ears was considered a wimp. Years later when I began to experience hearing loss in my left ear, the doctors traced the cause back to the 3 inch gun.

We docked at the Philadelphia navy yard and underwent a full refitting. I noticed the men from the shipyard performing work on the ship did so from work orders. Those of us on the bridge gang were supposed to chip and pant the deck of the bridge. I hated chipping paint. I had seen where the blank work orders were kept. Filtching one, I filled it out with an illegible signature. I put it in the work order box and waited to see what would happen. Lo and behold, a day later, a ship-yard work crew showed up and finished the job in a morning. The Exec showed up to check on us the next day. He was amazed at what we had accomplished, and congratulated us on a job well done.

I was a Quartermaster striker and stood navigation watch with the Exec. He and I got along. He encouraged me to take the Coast Guard Academy exam. I received word I'd passed it, but just then, I received word that my father had been killed in an accident in New Orleans.

I requested a transfer back to the 8th Coast Guard District to be closer to my mother. I was assigned to an 83 foot patrol boat on the Mississippi River. We spent a week at the mouth of the River responding to rescue calls and a week in port in New Orleans. Once, when on station at the River's mouth, we received a call from HQ that an airliner had gone down in the Gulf of Mexico. We were ordered to commence a search. A furious storm was pelting the area but off we went. We were out in the Gulf for hours searching a sector assigned to us.

The entire crew was seasick including the skipper, who had thirty years in the service. He was having trouble controlling the boat. He said it was down at the bow. He sent me below to check things out. I found seawater squirting into the head from the anchor locker. The skipper sent me and the Motormac forward with a gasoline-powered pump to the anchor locker. It was terrifying. The wind was howling and cold waves were breaking over us as we wrestled with the hatch. We discovered it hadn't been properly dogged down and that's how the sea water had gotten in. Then we had to get the pump started. It started right up thankfully and we were able to pump out the locker. When I got back aft I thought maybe a fox hole wouldn't be so bad. It turned out the airliner had crashed into the sea farther east just off of Mobile, Alabama. A cutter out of Mobile rescued several people.

On another occasion we took aboard a fisherman who had mangled his hand in a winch. He had lost a lot of blood and was in bad shape. We put in a call for an amphibian aircraft to transport him to a hospital. A Coast Guard Catalina arrived. On landing it was hit by a rogue wave and flipped over. It sank before our eyes with 5 crewmen aboard. We went as fast as we could to get the fisherman to a point where there was ground transportation to take him to a hospital. We never heard how he did.

The skipper was a Chief Boatswains Mate, an Irishman. When I reported aboard, he asked me if I could type. When I told him I could, he handed me a stack of mail. "You're in charge of mail from now on." He and I went through it. Some was up to a month old. We agreed that about three out of the stack needed answering. I wrote and typed the answers for him. He signed them and off they went.

The Chief didn't believe in all the paper work involved in requisitioning supplies. If we needed paint for example he sent us to the base paint locker to steal it. Thank God the cook requisitioned the food for the boat so we didn't go hungry.

Once when on station, thick fog covered the River. We were proceeding very slowly as we could not see anything. I was the bow lookout. I said to a shipmate who was just aft of me "I think I hear cow bells." My voice activated my microphone. The skipper heard me and shouted, "Report those cow bells!" So I did, "cow bells off the port bow." Shortly thereafter we plowed into the river bank. I was covered with willow branches and there was Bossy on the levee just off the bow nibbling at grass, and looking at us with absolutely no interest whatsoever.

Regularly when on station we pulled into the "Jump." This was a small port on the River with a grocery store and a bar. In addition to fresh produce, milk and such, we took on a case of beer or two which was charged off as tomatoes or whatever. From time to time, we would inspect the local shrimp boats for safety regulation compliance. When boarding we would put a bucket on the deck. Upon leaving the bucket would be full of shrimp. Boiled, they sure went well with the beer.

I took and passed the test as a Third Class Quartermaster and was assigned to the Coast Cutter Nike based in Gulfport Mississippi. The Nike's station when at sea was in Campeche Bay just off Mexico. The US shrimping fleet fished these waters and our principal task was to look after the shrimpers.

We encountered some pretty ferocious storms in the Gulf from time to time. One could end up black and blue from being thrown against bulkheads and ship's equipment when in high seas and wind. Once, I was on duty on the bridge watching the ship's inclinometer swing almost to the point of no return. Beyond this point, the ship rolls over and does not right it self.

We were at sea in such a storm one Thanksgiving Day. The cook was trying to roast a couple of turkeys. A few of us who were not on duty and not seasick were in the galley playing checkers. The cook was about to go bonkers checking on how the turkeys were doing. Timing was critical. He had to calculate when the ship was coming upright from a roll to unlock the ovens and poke a thermometer into the birds. On coming upright one time a rogue wave hit the ship and the turkeys flew out of the ovens. The turkeys were sliding every which way around the galley. We all joined in trying to catch them, burning hands on the hot greasy turkeys. When we finally cornered them, they were inedible. They were covered with filth from the bilges and galley deck. We had gravy sandwiches with cranberry sauce for Thanksgiving Dinner.

Most of the time when we were on patrol nothing happened. But from time-to-time we had an adventure. We got word from one of the shrimp boat crews that there was boat mixing in with the shrimp fleet that was not after shrimp. It was a floating bordello out of Florida. Its name was the "Bushwhacker." The Captain ordered the crew to be on the lookout for it.

The shrimpers fished at night, then anchored during the day and slept. Early one morning we approached a group of anchored shrimp boats. As we closed in one of the lookouts reported seeing the Bushwhacker. The Captain ordered us alongside. Several crewmen bordered her. They reported the cargo hold where shrimp were usually iced down was fitted out as a bar. Aft there were cribs, but there were no girls. The Captain went bonkers. He ordered us to keep a sharp look out for the girls, an order the crew had no problem carrying out. Later a guy who had been one of the lookouts when we first came upon the shrimp boats told me he saw the girls leaving the Bushwhacker by small boat and boarding another vessel. Then they shifted to another. He didn't report it to the bridge. This guy was not a fan of the Captain. I often wondered what the Captain was up to. The Coast Guard was not an international vice squad, and we had no jurisdiction over ships in international waters.

Gulfport was a sailor's delight. Sailor hangouts were not far from the ship. There was the moonshine dealer – a gallon for 5$. And there were girls.

The town lock-up was in walking distance. It was possible to bail out an inmate for five dollars or so, usually a farm girl from upstate Mississipp looking for adventure. She was in the slammer for vagrancy or shoplifting, or the like and she was yours for the night.

There was one hangout the USCGC Nike crew favored. I wish I could remember its name. Beer was reasonable and on Saturday nights there was music. Our 1st Class Boatswain's Mate Carlyle was a regular there and every body knew him. He was a big guy, over six feet tall and weighed a couple of hundred pounds, an amiable man from North Carolina.

Carlyle made himself forever memorable there when, after several pitchers of beer one night he returned from the head hung by the door jam in the bar; and swung back and forth with his fly still open. He created quite a sensation.

Well, one time to end all we pulled into port on a Saturday morning. After washing the ship down there was mail call. We saw Carlyle sitting with tears running down his cheeks. He had received a "dear John letter" from his North Carolina sweetheart. Carlyle was loved by all. His hurt, hurt us. Shipmatess came up to him and whispered condolences or just patted his arm, even the officers.

That night we corralled a group around Carlyle and headed to our favorite hang out. It was Saturday night and there was music. Carlyle ordered whiskey instead of beer.

The country group arrived and started to play. Carlyle requested "Dear John." Word had reached the band about Carlyle's loss. So they played it as sweetly as it could be played. Carlyle wept.

When they finished Carlyle shouted "Play it again!" So they did. The third time he shouted "Play it again" they gave him a very short version. The crowd understood.

But the forth time the leader said "Carlyle, No!"

Well, Carlyle rose out of his chair with God only knows how many whiskeys under his belt and attacked the band. He grabbed the guitar from the guitar player and smashed it over his head. The guitar player's head emerged from the wrecked guitar surrounded by strings. He then went after the drummer. A general fight broke out just like the ones you've seen in the movies. Chairs were thrown, tables were over turned. It was mainly the sailors against everybody else. We apparently won. We never went back to that bar again.

The Exec looked at all of us when we fell in the next morning with black eyes and what not but said not a word.

My three-year hitch ended in Gulfport. I said goodbye to my buddies, packed my sea bag and threw it into the harbor as I left. I headed back to New Orleans wiser somewhat more mature, and no longer a virgin.

Chapter 5. LSU

At LSU I came into my own. I partied and had a ball but I learned how to manage my time. I studied and made good grades. I received recognition. I became a leader.

Tuition was $150 a semester. The GI Bill provided $110 a month and with a job at the library providing another $50, money was no problem. Baton Rouge didn't have the diversions New Orleans did. I was challenged by what I was studying. I don't remember having a single mediocre professor. Some of them were outstanding. Dr. Erick Vogelein of the Government department has been referred to as one of the greatest thinkers of the 20th century.

I selected Government as my major. I was thinking of going on to grad school and becoming a professor or entering law school after I graduated. A friend of my father recommended Government. He told me it would teach me how to think.

I pledged DKE. Not having been initiated into KA at Tulane I was free to pledge other fraternities. The KA's at LSU were good guys, but I found more in common with the Dekes. They were super in every way. They knew how to party, but they also knew how to buckle down and get things done. Almost every year, DKE won the interfraternity Sweepstakes Trophy which combined scholastic achievement with athletic.

We drank at parties, but nobody passed out. Nancy was at LSU. She was two years younger but because of my three years in the Coast Guard she was a junior and I was a sophomore. We took up where we left off when I was at Tulane. Nancy graduated in 1956 a year ahead of me. I didn't have a car this time, but fraternity brothers were generous letting me use theirs.

I worked at the Government library mornings. Most of the students who studied there were grad students. They knew how to get what they wanted, so they seldom bothered me for anything. This meant I had the mornings to study. After lunch I studied for a couple more hours, and that did it. In the evenings I partied.

At the end of the first semester, I had straight A's. This made me something of a sensation in the fraternity house. My roommate was the only true genius in Deke. I figured some of his stuff must have rubbed off on me. He also introduced me to classical music. He had his record player and extensive collection of records in the dorm room we shared. It was on almost constantly. I decided I liked Mozart best.

LSU drinking rules were very different from Tulane's. Officially there was not supposed to be any alcohol at fraternity parties, but the rule was not enforced back then. If there was a drinking age law in Baton Rouge, it must have been 18. I don't remember ever being carded. Restaurants within a mile of the campus were prohibited from serving alcohol. This was dumb. All it did was discriminate against students without cars. Over the years I understand that rule was relaxed, but the administration has clamped down on drinking in the fraternity houses.

One of our hangouts just over the one-mile line was the Tiger Lounge. In addition to a bar and dance floor, there were pin ball

machines.   I was there one evening with a group of fraternity brothers.
Two of them were playing the pin balls for money. One of them was a
very bright, worldly law student. The other can only be described as the
fraternity's loser, a very nice, warm guy, but a loser.. He was notorious
for the amounts of money he lost at poker. He did things that made
him the object of jokes. Once suffering from hemorrhoids, he went
around campus carrying a doughnut pillow as if it were flag. Well the
law student was way ahead and the loser was way behind. They took a
break and went over to the bar to have a beer. The loser was lamenting
his losses. Just at that moment a roach walked across the bar (not
unusual for south Louisiana). The law student reached out and pinned
the roach to the counter by one of its legs.   "I'll forgive your debt if
you eat this roach." The loser didn't hesitate. He asked the bartender
for another beer and some crackers and catsup. He took over possession
of the roach; put it on a cracker covered it with catsup and downed it
in one gulp followed by most of a pint of beer. This story was all over
campus next day.

This was the year the Supreme Court handed down its decision on
Brown vs. the Board of Education which ended segregation in public
schools. There were several hundred black students at LSU then mostly
in grad school. The Louisiana legislature reacted by declaring all water
fountains and bathrooms at all public institutions "for whites only."
This was stupid. Where were the black students supposed to go? The
white students reacted. We tore down the signs wherever we saw them.
In the law library, someone put a sign on the oversized waste basket at
the desk "White Trash Only." The administration put the signs back
up no matter how many times we tore them down. Most of our parents
thought this was the right thing for them to do. Over the next few years
there were fewer and fewer black students at LSU until much later when
the South began to face reality.

At the end of my junior year, I was elected president of Deke. One didn't campaign for the position, but in the inevitable "whisper" campaign my roommate who was widely esteemed talked me up. I won. It was a great year learning how to steer this rambunctious gang. Just after my election, the Dean of Men asked me to come by his office. "Peter, we are going to have a conversation that I'll deny ever happened. It's about the real rules. I know you guys drink at the Deke house. That's OK, as long as it never becomes a public relations problem. I also know about the poker game on the second floor. That's OK, too. But let me make one thing absolutely clear. If I ever learn that a female student got drunk at the Deke house AND! was sexually abused. You, YOU! are dead meat, and I'll shut the house down.

The Dean didn't say anything about hazing pledges. He must have forgotten; but I enforced "no-paddling" of pledges and was supported by most everyone in the fraternity. We did have another problem, the Dean didn't touch. The pledges from New Orleans knew how to drink. Those from Louisiana's northern bible-belt didn't. They were on their own for the first time in their lives and having a ball. We had to watch them closely at rush parties. Some years, a few ended up in the infirmary with alcohol poisoning, but we had no disasters.

By my senior year, I had pretty much decided I was going on to grad school, get a Ph.D. in Government and follow the life of a college professor. I was awarded some honors. I was tapped by Omicron Delta Kappa, the national leadership honor society. Phi Kappa Phi, a national academic honor society invited me to join. LSU did not have an active Phi Beta Kappa chapter then because of the lack of a classics department. There was a group of Phi Beta Kappa professors at LSU who were working on establishing a chapter. While this was pending, they invited students who would have been initiated to a ceremony. We were presented with a letter to that effect. That was good enough for me.

I never failed to put down Phi Beta Kappa on resumes and was ready to answer any questions if they came up. They never did.

In my senior year, I passed the United States Foreign Service exam. A professor talked me in to taking it.When word came that I'd passed, I forgot all about grad school. The thought of being paid a regular salary instead of living the life of a student won me over. Right after graduation, I said my goodbyes and headed off to Washington DC.

Chapter 6. The Foreign Service

A. Washington

I arrived in Washington with one suitcase and a footlocker, all my worldly goods. I was introduced to another Foreign Service officer who was looking for someone to share an apartment. So I moved in. He was a great guy and we are still friends 48 years later. At the Foreign Service Institute (FSI) I followed a three-month orientation course. This included a two-week course on Consular application of U.S. immigration law. At the end of the orientation, some of us were assigned to Embassies and Consulates abroad; others were assigned to various offices in the Department of State. I was assigned to the Public Correspondence Branch of the Office of Public Affairs.

We answered the mail from the public to the Department of State and to the White House on foreign affairs. Our guidance on answering the mail came from the "desk" officers at State. To facilitate liaison with them, we were also organized as desks. I ran the Middle East desk. My hands were full when President Eisenhower ordered the Marines into Lebanon in 1958. There was a constant about the mail we received. Whenever US military units were deployed abroad, the mail was always predominantly negative. The people who were for it mostly didn't write.

A New York Times journalist called to ask how State's mail about the Lebanon landing was going. My boss, the Branch Chief explained how our mail was not an accurate indicator of the way Americans felt about things. The journalist said he didn't care. He said if we refused to release the numbers, he could make a story of that as well. Considering it the lesser of two evils, my boss gave him the numbers. The next morning, on the front page on the Times, there was an article sensationalizing how the mail to State overwhelmingly opposed the Lebanon landing.

Then Vice President Nixon told some reporters that he thought there was a communist in the State Department who had released the information on its mail to the press. My boss was in fact from a rock-ribbed Republican family in upstate New York. The Public Affairs Chief told him not to worry; State would protect him. Then Walter Winchel released his name on his radio program. My boss was apoplectic. The following day we attended the Secretary of State's regularly scheduled press conference. The question of the communist in the State Department came up. "Mr. Secretary, do you think there is a communist who released the mail numbers to the press?" the newsman asked. The Secretary replied biblically "By their acts ye shall know them." My boss slumped in his chair. The newsman got another question in "Sir, do you mean to leave the impression there is a communist in the State Department who is seeking to undermine American Foreign Policy?" "No I don't mean to leave that impression," the Secretary replied. My boss started breathing again.

For several days afterward, there were articles in the press about the "old" Nixon, referring to his communist hunting days. The year was 1958, not too long after the McCarthy era, and Nixon was then being touted as President Eisenhower's successor. In a few days with no further developments the press lost interest. Nothing untoward happened to my boss. Later he was assigned to a good post in Spain, and in due course he rose to the rank of Ambassador. I replaced him as Branch Chief.

One of my duties as Branch Chief was to attend the briefing of State's Press Secretary each morning. At that time it was Lincoln White, a tough old former press journalist. All the public affairs people and the USIS's representative were there. Lincoln White would arrive just having attended the Secretary of State's morning briefing. Linc, as he was called, covered the items from the Secretary's briefing that might provoke press inquiries, mail and the like. There were give-and-take discussions about how the hot items should be handled.

There was one guy always at the briefing who it was not clear who he was. The attendees I knew thought he must be CIA. In any case from time-to-time he proposed some recommendations even a junior FSO like me could tell were stupid. So one day after a briefing I got up the nerve to go up to Lincoln White and ask, "Can you tell me who the guy is who always sits on the far left side of the room?" He laughed and put his arm around my shoulder. "Peter that man is one of my most valuable advisors. He has the gift of always being wrong. You'd be surprised how many times the same dumb ass proposals come to me from the mouths of high level, highly experienced people who are more articulate, but I know immediately what to do with them." He gestured as though he were pulling a toilet chain. "Peter an advisor like that is almost as valuable as one who's always right."

Nancy and I were married in New Orleans. In thirteen months our daughter Suzy was born. As many young FSOs did, we lived in an apartment in Arlington VA.

I was sent to FSI to follow an intensive course in the Amharic language preparatory to an assignment to the Embassy in Ethiopia.

The course was nine months long and very tough. State's language instructors rank Amharic as one of the most difficult to learn on a par with Chinese. Following my language course, I was appointed U.S. Consul in Addis Ababa. My wife and I with our four- month-old daughter headed for Africa.

B. Ethiopia

My job as Consular officer was being the contact point between American citizens in Ethiopia and the US Government. This involved a lot of things: issuing passports and various other Consular documents, registering births and marriages of Americans, looking after the personal effects of Americans who had died in Ethiopia. I could offer Americans some support if they ran afoul of Ethiopian authorities, but in general private citizens were subject to the laws of Ethiopia. I also issued visas to Ethiopians and others who wanted to go the U.S.

We lived on the Embassy compound in what once was a stable. The property had been the estate of Empress Zauditu, Haile Selassie's aunt. I was told the Emperor gave it to President Roosevelt in appreciation for America's help liberating Ethiopia from the Italians in World War II. Such compounds are common in Third World countries where they are the security equivalent of "circling-the-wagons."

We had four servants: Yilma the cook, Bogale the houseboy, Adehni the mamita (nanny), and Gebre Mariam the gardener. Each of these people was from a different tribe. Yilma was Amhara, a member of the ruling tribe of Ethiopia. Bogale was Oromo (then called Galla), a member of the most populous tribe. Adehni was Tigre, a tribe closely related to the Amharas. Gebre Mariam was Gurage, a minority tribe that was sort of at the bottom of the heap. So there were six languages spoken in our house: Amharinya, Gallinya, Tigrinya, Guraginya, Italian which the servants mostly spoke to one another, and English.

This is the milieu in which our daughter Suzy spent her toddler-hood. She responded to all of these languages, but would only speak English. I guess she had figured out, she was of our tribe.

I was a Foreign Service officer (FSO) of grade 7, second then from the bottom rung of the officer ladder. I made $7700 a year. I didn't have to pay rent for the stable. That was part of an FSO's package, but I did have to pay the salaries of all our servants. One evening, I counted the number of people in our "extended family". Including the servants and their families, the total was 16! Was I really responsible for the welfare of this many people? I felt overwhelmed.

An extended family we did become, certainly in so far as Suzy and later David were concerned. They spent as much time with these people as they did with Nancy and much more for sure than they did with me. I wouldn't know how to begin to judge the extent of their influence in the rearing of our children, but I have no regrets no matter how much that might have been. These were all admirable people. Being a domestic servant particularly for a *tilik getoch - a lord (me?)* was not a low-level position in Ethiopia. Status was not determined by what a person did for a living anyway. Much more important, were such traditional factors as tribe or clan family, and standing in these. "Standing" was something earned. This was as true in the other African and Asian countries where we later lived, as it was in Ethiopia back then.

Yilma boiled and filtered our drinking water. An ancient ceramic water filter made in England in the early part of the century sat on a counter top. A kettle boiled away on the range. Yilma topped up the filter from time-to-time from the kettle. The USAID water people had drilled a well on the compound behind the Ambassador's residence that yielded potable water, but not enough to supply the compound on a daily basis. The Military Assistance Advisory Group (MAAG) had a tanker truck that filled up weekly at the well and distributed the water to the MAAG families in Addis. I once asked the Embassy Administrative Officer why the truck didn't drop off some of the potable water to Embassy families while it was in the neighborhood. He informed me, "Peter when in Africa in the Foreign Service, one boils one's water to drink. The Ambassador boils his water and the well is in his back yard. You'll boil yours too."

Cocktail parties were a mainstay in the Diplomatic Service. They were a handy way to introduce visitors to a lot of Ethiopians at one function, useful for repaying hospitality and they were over relatively quickly. In my early years in the Foreign Service, I thought they were fun. Later I avoided them when I could. I much preferred a lunch or dinner where one could sit around a table and have time to talk, and eat! Suzy liked the cocktail parties. She would come in to greet early guests in her robe and pajamas, shining from Adehni's scrubbing in the bath. After Suzy was supposed to have gone to bed, it was common during the evening to see a little hand coming up from under the hors d'oeuvres table reaching for some favorite cocktail snack. Our son David was born in Addis Ababa at a missionary hospital a year after we arrived.

The Emperor dominated the city. One was constantly reminded of his presence by his regal comings and goings. He was driven about at a stately pace in a splendid old Daimler car with guards and outriders fore and aft. The custom upon encountering the Emperor's entourage on the street was to immediately pull over, dismount from your car, stand facing the Daimler and bow as he went past

When the Peace Corps arrived in Ethiopia, the Ambassador took me along to the ceremony when the group was presented to Haile Selassie. I was one of the first FSO's trained in Amhariniya. I was decked out in my morning suit, cutaway coat and striped trousers. After offering his greetings, the Ambassador presented me to the Emperor. I bowed and said "Ten'astelin- Girmawi Hoy."(Greetings, Your Imperial Majesty).

Haile Selassie smiled at me. "Amhariniya yaukalu!"(Ah! You speak Amharinya) he exclaimed. "I can speak some, Your Imperial Majesty," I responded in Amhariniya. "Bet'am t'iru no!"(Very good) he said, and beamed at the Ambassador. Made my day.

Virtually everywhere outside of Addis when we lived there, was referred to as the "bush" by the expatriates. Bush is defined in Webster's New Collegiate Dictionary as "a large uncleared or sparsely settled area." West toward Lake T'ana and the Blue Nile gorge were forested mountains with scattered villages of farmers' tukuls (the traditional Amhara round dwelling of chica and straw roof.) Toward the south-west one descended into rain forest. Toward the east from Addis one descended into the Rift Valley and the Danakil Desert. Toward the south the descent was into the Arusi Desert, typical African savannah of acacia trees and scrub brush, and the Rift Valley lakes. The settlement pattern in the south was one of crude huts made from scrub brush surrounded by thorn fences. There were few large villages. One mostly saw small compounds of several families. The Arusi people kept goats and hunted. This is where we went camping most of the time. On our first camping trip, we did it the typical American way. We and another Embassy family drove down to Lake Langano, one of the Rift Valley lakes. We took cooking utensils from our kitchens, kerosene lanterns, ice chests of food and drink, and our kids. We froze cans of beer so they would stay cold longer. We cooked over a Coleman stove, ate at a folding camp table, washed dishes with sand at the edge of the lake, slept on the ground in sleeping bags and thought we were having a good time.

My British counterpart Ronnie Peel and his family were camped a couple of miles away on the same lake. Lake Langano was the preferred lake because it was *believed* not to harbor the snails that were hosts to the deadly liver fluke that caused schistosomiasis. The other Rift Valley lakes were thought to be infected. Ronnie, the British Consul, had been in Ethiopia since the end of WWII. He had swum in Lake Langano for some fifteen years, and had yet to come down with the disease. We all watched him closely for signs of declining health. A uniformed guard from the British Embassy arrived in our camp one afternoon with an invitation from my friend to come over and join the Brits for cocktails. We scrubbed off in the lake and drove over to their camp.

It was a revelation for us to see the way the Brits *camped*. The guards presented arms as we entered the camp gate. A shaven Ronnie greeted us and showed us around the compound. There was a large dining tent with table and chairs, a white linen tablecloth, silver candlesticks and places set with crystal and silver cutlery for the evening meal. There were several sleeping tents equipped with camp beds, chests of drawers, and Persian carpets on the ground. There was a bath enclosure, a loo (British toilet), and the piece de resistance, a drinking canopy pitched at the lake's edge.

Beckoning us to the canopy, Ronnie asked if we would like martinis. After we settled in the easy chairs of the canopy with our feet dangling in the lake, a waiter in white arrived with a pitcher of martinis with *ice!* They had a portable camp fridge! A rare item in those days. I complemented our host on his set-up. He looked at me over his glasses and remarked "Well you know, Peter, any damned fool can make himself uncomfortable." We all nodded agreement as we raised our glasses as if at communion, and sipped in quiet appreciation.

Once when camping in the Nile River gorge, we came upon a pair of baboons copulating in the middle of the road down to the river. They scrambled away casting angry baboon curses at us for the intrusion. On our return, a couple of hours later, the driver mentioned we were approaching the spot where we had seen the baboons. No one thought we would see the couple again, but there they were, still at it. They were really mad this time. They shook their fists at us.

Another time we went camping at a hot spring east of Addis Ababa. It was a lovely spot. However, we found sitting in the hot water enervating. A doctor later told us this was probably because of atomic activity in the spring. No one noticed lots of mosquitoes, but on our return Nancy came down with malaria. Several other people who had been on the trip also did. Fortunately Suzy didn't and neither did I.

A final camping story. I was recovering from hepatitis. The doctor suggested a two-week rest away from Addis Ababa. Even though the Cuban Missile crisis was brewing, there wasn't anything any of us in Ethiopia could do about it. So, I loaded up the kids, three servants including Yilma, Adehni and a driver, all our stuff and headed down to Lake Langano. Occasionally we were able to tune in to barely audible BBC and VOA reports and follow events. I remember thinking that if the world were going to blow up, we were probably as well off as anyone at Lake Langano with our little family together in the place where mankind had originated.

Power has never passed in a peaceful, straight forward, Western-type manner from one regime to the other in Ethiopia. For centuries, members of the royal family schemed and fought against one another to capture the throne. At times in the country's early history sitting rulers banished their competitors to a remote guarded mountain top, and had them closely guarded to head off succession schemes. Nowadays, since Emperor Haile Selassie's overthrow by the military, which is the current pattern in Africa, competition for power occurs among commoners. Haile Selassie himself overthrew his cousin in 1916, and ruled as the regent for his aunt, Empress Zauditu until 1930. He became Emperor after the Empress died under suspicious circumstances. When we arrived Haile Selassie had been in power for almost forty-five years.

The Emperor ruled with an iron fist as absolute monarch. Noblemen appointed by the Emperor headed the Imperial Bodyguard. There was a large Army Air Force and small Navy each supported and trained by different foreign powers. The US supported the Army; the Swedes and US the Air Force; the Danes the navy; the Brits the Imperial Bodyguard; and the Israelis the intelligence service. The Russians were busy trying to penetrate any and all of these. The Ethiopian church controlled most of the arable land. The Emperor deftly played off everyone against the other. Modernizing forces were at work in the Ethiopia of the 1960's encouraged, but tightly controlled by the Emperor. Young men were returning to the country from government-sponsored education abroad. Foreign concepts such as land reform and democracy were being quietly discussed among them. In December 1960, the commander of the Imperial Bodyguard decided to take action. While the Emperor was away on state visits to Latin America, Colonel Menghistu led a revolt against the throne. The Bodyguard took over the main positions of power in Addis. They commenced negotiations to win the support of the other military forces. At this point all was fairly quiet in the city. The Bodyguard's spokesman on the radio, talked about the coming of democracy and land reform. The Crown Prince added words of support (later said to have been coerced from him). Foreign diplomats dashed about conferring, and watching and waiting, and trying to determine which way to jump. The cars of the various ambassadors kept arriving at our compound. After a day or so, the negotiations broke down, and the other military forces attacked the Bodyguard in support of the Emperor. The Bodyguard made hostages of most of the Emperor's ministers who had not gone with him, and fell back on the Emperor's palace just down the street from the American Embassy. At the outbreak of the fighting in mid-morning, the army started lobbing artillery shells at the palace. As they zeroed in, the Embassy began to receive some of the long shots on the compound. We also received some stray strafing fire from attacking planes. Our Marines took up defensive positions around the Embassy compound. Over the next couple of days, the loyalist forces closed in on the rebels. As it became clear the loyalists were going to prevail, the rebel leaders asked the Ambassador to come to the palace to help them try to work out a cease fire. He, the US Army attaché, and the CIA station chief had just arrived at the palace when, Army tanks broke through the palace's main gate. A rebel officer urged the Ambassador to leave immediately. He escorted them to a rear window. As they jumped to the ground they heard machine gun fire behind them. The rebels were executing the hostages. There was no sign of the Ambassador's car and driver, but there sat a Palace sedan of uncertain make and vintage. The Ambassador saw the keys in the ignition. He slipped into the driver's seat and the others leapt in beside him. The Ambassador cranked, gunned the engine, and off they went through a back gate opened by the Palace staff as they fled. It was a close call. The CIA station chief who was normally a teetotaler, downed several robust scotches that evening when he joined us at the stable. The Ambassador's driver made it back safely to the compound. I don't know what ultimately happened to the palace car our Ambassador commandeered. During lulls in the fighting, Americans had streamed in to the Embassy compound. Those of us living there took them in. We had wall-to-wall people in the stable. Nancy and Yilma served over two hundred meals during the three days of fighting. Following the attack on the palace and the capture of the coup's leaders, the rebels began to scatter, and the coup collapsed, but Addis was still a war zone for weeks afterward. Gunfire chattered on day and night as loyalist troops sought out and shot hiding Bodyguard personnel. The Ethiopian Army troops badgered the local population for "gifts" as they went about this business. The Emperor returned. In an online telex "conversation" with the Ambassador after he landed at the US military base in Eritrea, Haile Sellasie asked if it were safe for him to come to Addis. The Ambassador earned his pay that day. He turned to those of us in the telex room with him and commented to the effect, how the hell am I supposed to know if it is safe for the Emperor to return to the capitol of his Empire following a revolt by his own bodyguard? He thought for a moment, shrugged, and sent a positive reply. The population turned out in the thousands to welcome the Emperor home. Men waved tree branches and the women ululated as he drove by in his Daimler. The atmosphere was biblical.

As all of this wound down, we prepared to celebrate our first Christmas in Ethiopia. Nancy managed to get hold of a few spindly conifer tree branches. She had Gebre Mariam tie them together so they faintly resembled a Christmas tree. I made a train for Suzy from wood and Klim powdered milk cans. Nancy found a small wicker table and child's plastic tea service in the market. We drove downtown on Christmas afternoon to see if anything was going on. What was going on was the displaying of the bodies of Bodyguard soldiers hanging from lampposts in the main square. For months after the coup whenever a low flying plane passed over the stable, Suzy would cock an ear to the sky and quickly crawl under the nearest table. She would just sit there calmly and wait until the sound faded away. Adehni had taught her to do this. No doubt it was something she had learned as a child when the Italians invaded Ethiopia in the 1940's. We stopped taking notice of this trick and in time Suzy stopped doing it. David being in the womb at the time, showed no ill effects upon his arrival. We worked hard at getting to know Ethiopians, mainly young western-educated professionals. They came to the stable often to drink our American beer (I preferred the Ethiopian beer) and to relax and speak freely. The Emperor had lots of secret police and they closely watched the young professionals. We knew our phones were tapped because a US-educated electrical engineer friend, who worked in the Ethiopian telephone company, told us so. The Marines periodically swept our house for bugs. Suzy and David got a lot of attention from these Ethiopian friends. Suzy was Suzina and David was Dawit. Some of them joined us camping. It was not a thing they normally did. What they really enjoyed was conversation. Shortly after the coup, I was moved to the political section.. My principal assignment in this new job was to get to know these young Ethiopian professionals and keep abreast of what they were thinking. After the coup, the young Amharas began to think a lot about what Col. Menghistu had been trying to accomplish. He had been captured tried and executed in the wake of the coup. We had some fascinating discussions about the Emperor, did he provide good leadership or bad? If he went, what would work in his place? They agreed that if the Bodyguard had succeeded, it might have been pretty much more of the same. There was some talk that communism might be the only means of reforming Ethiopia. I told the Ambassador about the sort of conversations that were going on late at night in the stable. He told me to press on, but to be careful not to imply any sort of US support for moves to overthrow the Emperor. Keep the discussions "seminar-like" he urged. As far as I could tell, the young professionals were not in touch with their counterparts in the military in any political way in those days. It was many years later that the movement came that unseated the Emperor and overturned the power of the Church. Sergeants and junior officers in the Army, who were mostly from the Galla tribe led this movement. They had a Marxist orientation and they didn't waste any time killing, imprisoning or causing the educated Amharas to flee the country. Although the Marxists are now gone, the Amharas have not resumed power. The Tigres who fought for years to overthrow the Amharas, led the group that drove out the Marxists.   There is no Emperor, but a monolithic presidency; *plus ca change ...*

It was time to pack up again. I was assigned to the Embassy in Kuala Lumpur, Malaya as political officer.

C. Malaya

Kuala Lumpur (KL) the capitol of then Malaya means "muddy river confluence" in Behasa Melayu, the language of Malaya. It was a charming and truly exotic place, a magical mixture of East and West. Some of the public buildings must have inspired Walt Disney. British colonial administrators amused themselves over the years designing buildings with the *Arabian Nights* in mind. Juxtaposed against these fanciful Eastern structures in the center of the city was a Gothic Anglican cathedral, a Tudor-style British Club, statuary of British royalty and a cricket pitch. Just a block over was the beginning of a high-rise modern city center. Another block away, was a street scene from anywhere in China. There was a European residential area of colonial villas. Surrounding all this were traditional Malay kampongs, villages of wooden houses on stilts amid banana trees with painted white rocks bordering beds of flowers, and swept dirt paths. Mixed in and among the kampongs were the "council" type houses the Government provided the Indians who mostly worked for the railroad in KL.

At first we lived in the European residential area in one of the few apartment buildings found among the villas. Our apartment had three bedrooms and servants' quarters. Ah Yick the cook; his wife Jum Eng, the Amah (all purpose maid and nanny) and their 10-year-old son, Ah Li An, occupied the servants' quarters. Ah Yick was a taciturn old Chinese gentleman who shuffled around never seeming to lift his heels. He could produce wonderful Western as well as Asian meals. It was hard to tell what age he was, anywhere from forty to sixty we guessed. Jum Eng was sunshine and laughter. The children adored her. She was shocked that they were not yet potty trained. She glanced at Nancy with barely concealed disdain, brooking no excuses about constant moves and such. She took over, and it was handled in a week. Ah Li An was a Chinese schoolboy who spent a lot of time studying. When he had some spare time, he played with Suzy and David. They thought Ah Li An was great. We had formed another nice extended family.

Shortly after our arrival, we were visited by a snake charmer. The snake charmer appeared one Sunday afternoon in our garden. Our apartment was on the ground floor, and our living room terrace opened right onto the garden. He was a thin, elderly Indian gentleman, dressed like Mahatma Ghandi. A round, covered basket sat on the ground next to him. The basket sort of shivered slightly from time to time. The snake charmer had probably been sitting in our garden for some moments observing us before we noticed him. When we did, he bowed and asked if we were interested in some amusement. Nancy and I looked at one another and thought "What the heck we're in Malaya." So at ages three and two, Suzy and David were treated to watching a hooded cobra swaying back and forth a few feet away on their living room floor, to the music of the old man's flute. I would say, having no idea of what a cobra was, they were only moderately interested. Nancy and I were fascinated.

Then, we were burglarized. I awoke one morning, and went about the living and dining rooms trying to find where I had put my watch. At about the time, I began to notice some things out of place. Jum Eng burst out of the kitchen telling me we had been burgled. Sure enough burglars had entered the apartment during the night. They came in through the front door by simply pushing the key back through the lock with a piece of wire. The key fell on a piece of paper they had put in under the door. They then pulled back the piece of paper picked up the key, unlocked the door and stealthily entered the house. While waiting for the police to come, we followed their tracks. They fished Ah Yick's trousers off the bedpost of the bed he and Jum Eng were sleeping in and took his wallet. They went into our "go down" and took the Scotch whisky, brandy and other stuff they recognized, leaving behind the bourbon. They went into each of Suzy and David's bedrooms and sat on the other twin bed in the rooms as they went through the loot they had gathered. You could see the impression on the beds where they had sat. In addition to my watch and some other odds and ends, they had taken my car key. All of this went on while we were asleep in our beds! I looked outside. The car was still there. In order to go outside, I had to unlock the front door. The burglars with great consideration, had locked the door on their way out and slid the key back under the door into the house.

The polite Malay policeman described to us all that must have happened, how they got in, what they were after, and who they probably were. He told us, slightly built Indians stripped themselves almost naked and greased their bodies so they could easily slip away if someone awoke and tried to capture them. There had been reports of them spraying some concoction into the air-conditioning vents to assure their victims stayed asleep. He told us these people were specialists. They would not come back to steal our car but they would sell the keys to others who would. He also said the police would do their best, but it was quite unlikely we would recover anything. I asked if the Indian snake charmer had been an accomplice. Had he cased the place for the subsequent burglary? Probably, said the Malay policeman. "These Indian burglars are very clever." For some reason, the VW dealer had to replace the one key I had with three, one for the ignition, one for the hood, and one for the engine compartment.

Malaya was a former British colony, and a rich one. It was then the world's leading supplier of natural rubber and tin ore. The British found the native Malays, whose traditional occupation was either fishing or rice farming, unwilling to engage in the hard work required to tap rubber trees, or mine for tin, so they imported Indians to do the former and Chinese to do the latter.

The three major ethnic groups shared power in a delicately balanced system left to them by the departing British colonial rulers in 1960. A coalition of Muslim Malays, Buddhist Chinese, Hindu and Muslim Indians, with a sprinkling of Christians between the latter two groups, governed the country. Several opposition parties pursued narrow ethnic interests. When we arrived, this was the principal political dynamic at work in the country. The other was an effort by the British to withdraw from other former colonies in the area. Malaya became Malaysia in 1963 by the addition of former British colonies Singapore at the tip of the Malay Peninsular and Sabah and Sarawak on the island of Borneo. The country had a king, the Yang di Pertuan Agong. This ceremonial position was rotated among the sultans of the nine traditional Malay States. The government was a British-type parliamentary democracy headed by a prime minister. The two houses of parliament were elected by universal suffrage. Malays dominated the military and police, the Chinese the economy, and the Indians the labor unions.

The chief of the Embassy Political Section was a senior FSO with long experience in Southeast Asia and fluent in Behasa Melayu. The number two was a Chinese language FSO which meant he spoke fluent Mandarin Chinese and had experience in China and Southeast Asia. So these two shared responsibility for keeping tabs on the majority party. I as the junior political officer had the opposition parties pretty much to myself. I studied Behasa Melayu with an instructor each day.

A general election was scheduled for 1964, the first since independence. Lee Kwan Yu, the dynamic young leader of Singapore and his mostly Chinese party were going to be a major factor in the elections for the first time. It was an exciting time to be there. I asked the Embassy to let me move out of the European residential area in KL, to a new suburb Petaling Jaya (PJ). PJ was becoming the home of many Malay, Chinese and Indian professionals. Among our neighbors was the nephew of the leader of the major opposition Malay political party, himself a junior officer in the Malay Foreign Service. Just behind our house lived the leader of one of the opposition Chinese political parties, a fellow named Choo Choo Soot. An Indian journalist, on one of the principal opposition newspapers, who became a friend, lived down the street.

The news of President Kennedy's assassination reached us in Malaysia. People in downtown KL went about with tears in their eyes, all of them Malays Chinese and Indians. They grabbed my hand as I walked down the street, tears flowing and told me how sorry they were. I didn't know I was so recognizable as an American. We were a global extended family mourning the vital, young American President. He seemed somehow someone close to all of us. I returned to the Embassy in tears. Nancy had the same experience in PJ.

Suzy and David attended a preschool, their first of many schools. Suzy liked it but David preferred staying home with Jum Eng. He was her favorite. Nancy often had to remind her to pay more attention to Suzy. Asia then was a man's world, and it was pretty much made that way by women who catered to them.

Malaysia is a small country, slightly larger than New Mexico. We never got to Sarawak and Sabah, the parts of the country on the island of Borneo, but we traveled the Malay Peninsula from one end to the other. The Straits of Malacca are on the west coast of the country between it and Indonesia. The South China Sea is on the east coast. Mountains form a spine running down the peninsula. The island of

Singapore is at the very southern tip. No camping here. We stayed in hotels, villas and government guesthouses.

On weekends, we often rented villas owned by various trading companies on the Straits of Malacca, or in the mountains nearby. All came equipped with their own servants. We used to travel a lot with a British friend, Dr. Peter Chapman and his wife and two children the same ages and sexes as ours. He was the contract Embassy physician. This was a comfort when they and their children and we and ours swam in beautiful mountain streams that were supposed to be avoided because of the suspected presence of whatever it is that causes the dreaded Leptospirosis.

At one of the "hill stations" as they were called by the British, we stayed at a hotel where there were signs in the corridors, "Children Will Be Quiet Between the Hours of One and Four PM.." No one spoke above a whisper in a cozy room with a fireplace where we gathered for drinks before dinner. Some of the guests quietly read years-old issues of *Country Life*. We wore jackets and ties. In the dining room there were a number of tables for one. There were no children present as they had their tea at five and were now in bed. For amusement one took walks and read. It was a great place for those who sought peace and quiet. We only went there once.

The scenery on the east coast of Malaysia was among the most beautiful we had ever seen. There were mountains to the west and unspoiled palm-fringed beaches to the east, for miles and miles. There were no bridges then and we crossed the many rivers flowing from the mountains to the sea by ferry. There were no hotels. The only places to stay overnight were the government guesthouses. There was no air conditioning. The bedrooms were equipped with mosquito nets and the baths were Malay "mandis," huge ceramic jars from which you dipped water to pour over your head to bathe.

47

The European food served at all of these places was unbelievably bad. The mainstay, something called "chicken chop" was a piece of dried-out chicken that had been smashed with a mallet, coated with flour and then fried. This was served almost cold with sticky mashed potatoes and English peas that were like little green rocks. We quickly learned to opt for the Malay dishes which were great, *nasi goring* (fried rice) and all sort of curries.

Once, we returned from the east coast to KL by putting our car on the flatcar of a train that went across the peninsula through the mountains. This was a trading train that carried goods from the coast. There were fresh fish and staples of various kinds displayed on the wooden seats of the third-class coaches. The train would stop whenever anyone stepped out of the jungle and waved it down. Raw rubber and jungle fruit of all kinds took the place of the fish as we proceeded. The engine was coal burning. As we passed though dozens of tunnels the engineer would give a warning toot so you could hold your breath to avoid choking on the smoke. The dining car was a freight car where squatting men cooked fish and *nasi goreng* on charcoal braziers. Suzy and David loved the whole experience. We went from one end of the train to the other scrambling over piles of raw rubber and sampling exotic fruit. We passed banks of wild orchids growing within reach out the open coach windows. When we reached the terminus at Kuala Lipis that evening we dumped both kids into the mandi at the guesthouse. It took quite a bit of scrubbing to get them clean.

On a west coast trip one time we stopped for lunch on a Sunday at a Chinese hotel in one of the small towns. We were greeted warmly and seated in the dining room which was empty. In time older men accompanied by young attractive women began to descend the stairs and join us. Suzy remarked how pretty all the young women were.

Some of them tousled David's hair and winked at me as they passed our table. I tried to keep my eyes on my food. Nancy was amused. The food was excellent.

I received a commendation from the State Department for my reporting on the general election. This was a good thing for a young Foreign Service officer. When I was in Ethiopia, I had requested university training in African studies. State was seeking to build a bench of area specialists. My selection came through while we were in Malaysia, and I was sent to UCLA for a year of academic studies in the history, politics, economy, anthropology and so on of Africa. We had loved Ethiopia; and during the Kennedy administration, Africa was an area of great interest. The African Bureau of the Department of State wanted me, so I signed on. But we were sorry to leave Malaysia.

D. African Studies at UCLA

Living in Westwood Village on the edge of the UCLA campus was a great experience. Suzy and David were introduced to living in their home country for the first time. I pointed out to them that southern California was a little bit different from the rest of the country. One day while walking to Baskin Robbins, we encountered a totally naked woman strolling down the middle of the street. We went swimming in the Pacific Ocean and visited the magic kingdom of Disneyland. I shipped my 1948 MG-TC back to the States. We tooled around LA in it with the top down. Suzy and David sat scrunched on crossed legs on the little back shelf. We stayed off of freeways. The MG just wasn't up to that.

I found UCLA's African Studies graduate program fascinating. Since I'd been in college eight years before, government or political science as it was called at UCLA had undergone major changes. I didn't recognize the discipline. It had been taken over by sociologists, statisticians and mathematicians. Professors were devising mathematical formulas to signify political stability and such. It seemed hooey to me, and really didn't help analysis or understanding very much. However, I learned to play the game and even produced a paper that drew on set theory to explain the modernizing process in Nigeria. Another more traditional paper I wrote, was published by UCLA in a collection of papers presented by graduate students at a colloquium on Africa.

Also fascinating, was witnessing the birth of the American student protest movement. At Berkeley, a student named Mario Savio climbed up on the hood of a car and gave a speech to students at the University of California on student rights to free speech on campus. When he climbed back down, things were never the same again at US colleges. Heretofore, students were considered wards of the university, and controllable as such including what they could say publicly. Now they were "citizens" just like any other, and free to speak for or against anything, anytime, anywhere. I watched the movement spread down south to UCLA. The students struck me as being fairly level headed. At first, they were wary of the more extreme positions being advocated. It was the professors who were the rabble-rousers, particularly when it came to the Vietnam War.

We passed a pleasant nine months in California. Then we left for Washington and three months of intensive French language training preparatory to an assignment as economic officer at the Embassy in Yaounde, Cameroon in West Africa.

On the QE 2:Capt., me, Jack, Kate, Suzy and Greg

High School Graduates: David 80', Suzy 79'

Nancy, me and somebody's cat in Saudi Arabia.

Kate

Suzy and Greg

David and Anne

Jack

Lindsay at her favorite Japanese Restaurant

Agent Matey's handler

Agent Matey

The G Kids

"And booked in all the finest clubs are................."

E. Cameroon

We traveled about southern France on our way to Marseille to join a ship which took us around the west coast of Africa to Cameroon. On our journey through France, we followed the advice of a Foreign Service friend who had long experience in dining with children in French restaurants. We ordered them an omelet. It was always good and came fast. The waiters understood. Then they ate tidbits from our meals when they came. It surprised them to discover they liked some of our food. In time they asked for a serving of this or that to follow their omelet. By the end of the trip they were jaded gourmets. Suzy liked pate, David liked escargots.

The State Department travel office at first objected to my request to take a ship from France to Cameroon. They said it was not the normal thing to take a ship on the way *to* a posting in Africa. Usually people did it on their return. I pointed out that as a French-speaking Africanist, chances were I would be spending a lot of my career in West Africa. I would like to have a look at the place on my way out to my first posting in the area. Besides I was using my own leave time to cover the ten-day's travel time en route. The travel office reluctantly agreed and booked the Juge family from Marseilles to Douala Cameroon on the M/V *Le General Mangin,*, one of the French passenger, mail and cargo liners.

These ships were throwbacks to the heyday of European colonialism. They were the essential transportation link between the home country and the African colonies. Their day was almost over as air travel was taking their place. We wanted to experience that phase of the continent's history and pass the remainder of our home leave having a look at our likely future. The itinerary of port calls was Casablanca, Dakar, Freetown, Conakry, Abidjan, Tema, Porto Novo, Lagos, and Douala.

The ship itself went on to ports in Congo (Brazzaville) and Zaire. It returned to Marseille via some of the same ports and some others.

There were comfortable cabins once reserved for the European colonial masters, now occupied about evenly by Europeans and members of the African elite. African traders and their families were crowded into passenger spaces on the main deck of the ship. Constant smells of cooking, sounds of conversation, laughter and babies crying rose up from this area to the cabin passenger decks above.

There were two sittings in the dining room. The early one was at 6 PM for children and elderly passengers and the second at 8 PM for everyone else. Nancy and some of the other mothers oversaw the children's' meal. At Suzy and David's table there was a little French boy about Suzy's age. He was always by himself and got help from Nancy or the waiter when he needed it. He always had a glass of watered-down wine with his meals. Suzy and David had milk. They were served courses and got pretty much the same thing we did later. Their French table companion was an expert at separating his fish from the bone with knife and fork. Suzy and David were impressed and duly learned how themselves. While Nancy was attending the children I was in the bar joining shipmates (including most of the European mothers) for cocktails. Those were different times. After the children finished eating they went off to the nursery and Nancy joined us in the bar where she had a "whisky telephone" waiting for her. This was the French bartender's little joke for the English-speaking passengers, "whisky et l'eau."

We were placed at a table with the German Ambassador to Senegal and his wife and the wife of the French Ambassador to Togo. They were all returning to post from home leave. They were very nice people particularly in smoothly switching into English when they could sense our newly acquired French was being challenged. We learned a lot about Africa from them.

The meals were outstanding. It *was* a French ship. Wine came with the meals in the form of a bottle each of Bordeaux Rouge and Bordeaux Blanc placed automatically on the table at the beginning of the meal. Empties were refilled. A wine menu was available for those who wanted something better, but I never saw anyone order from it. After all, these people were mostly all civil servants who were used to living within allowances. The businessmen who might have ordered from the wine list were not on the plodding old *General Mangin*. They were flying first class in airplanes thousands of feet above us.

Nancy and I got to meet a wide variety of quite interesting people on this voyage, mostly Europeans and Africans. The only other American on the ship was the wife of the United States Information Service director for Ghana who was returning from home leave. I particularly enjoyed the company of an elderly Ivoirien gentleman who told me jokes in French. We puzzled our young European friends as we did not join them in the lounge for dancing after collecting our children from the nursery following dinner. We Americans of course were afraid our children might sleep walk or something and fall overboard, so we stayed with them in the cabin. The Europeans simply put the kids down in their cabins and headed for the lounge. One fellow passenger, the Austrian Consul in Nigeria mentioned to me with just the hint of a leer that he and his wife were curious to know what we found to do so early in the evening after the children went to sleep. Many Europeans I found over the years took pleasure in tweaking Americans whom they thought were all naifs with such comments. They hoped for blushing, tongue-tied "Gary Cooper-type" responses they could regale their "sophisticated" compatriots with. I winked at the Consul, and he beamed.

Our trips ashore at the ports we visited revealed much of a sameness. There were the same market scenes, the same vast divisions between rich and poor, the same petty officials throwing their weight around and the same soldiers with guns. At one stop we saw day laborers who were hired to carry off passengers' baggage fighting over the leftovers from room service breakfasts in departing passengers' cabins. These people were *really hungry*. Meanwhile at each port the traders on deck were doing a brisk business trading liters, yes liters, of "French" perfume for all sorts of local goods. All of these images were entirely superficial, but all so much *alike*.

After a week on *Le General Mangin*, Nancy and I agreed we had fallen under a sort of spell. It was as if time stood still. The routine of daily activities: fine meals; kids' nursery; bridge; being waited on; port visits; "whisky telephones;" and interesting conversations segued in front of us like a movie we could watch forever! We finally arrived at Douala the main port of the country of Cameroon. We were supposed to connect that day with a flight to Yaounde the capital, but we learned the flight was canceled. The Air Cameroon agent frankly told us there were too few passengers to make the trip worthwhile. They would fly the next day. "Where are you putting us up for the night?" I asked. "Not us," he said. "This is not an interrupted connecting flight." The agent of the Nouvelle Compagnie des Paqueboats said it was not his lookout either. The ship had arrived on time. I knew the State Department wasn't going to pay. So yet once again our status as "migrant workers and itinerant performers" (how the IRS categorized FSOs) meant we were out-of-pocket for traveling expenses. The spell of *Le General Mangin* began to dissipate.

Cameroon, the "old coasters" (Europeans with long years of service on the African west coast) say, is located in the "armpit" of Africa. The Germans first colonized the area during the late 19th century European "scramble for Africa," and held it for about twenty years. After WWI the League of Nations took the colony from the defeated Germans and parceled it out as spoils of war between France and the United Kingdom. The British incorporated their piece into their West African colony of Nigeria. France set its piece up as the separate French colony of Cameroon. When Cameroon gained its independence from France in 1960 the southern part of the former German colony that had been annexed to Nigeria rejoined Cameroon having become tired of being treated as a stepchild by Lagos.

So then we had a newly independent country with 24 major African language groups, two official languages, French and English, and vestigial usage of yet another European language, German. The new Cameroonian Government had designs on the adjacent Spanish colony of Spanish Guinea sometimes called Fernando Po. The Spanish were in the process of unloading their African colonies then. Had the Cameroonians succeeded (they didn't) the new Cameroon would have been unique in the Third World, with speakers of more European languages than even Switzerland i.e. French, English, German and Spanish.

We lived in Yaounde. Cameroon was a typical West African country with major export crops of cocoa and coffee. Petroleum exploration had only just begun. Their major import from the United States then was used clothes. The French still ran the place. It was their "chase garde," private hunting ground. We lived in a neighborhood of villas occupied by European diplomats and the Cameroonian elite. It had only recently been converted from grazing land. Herders still led their cattle through the streets and open areas between the houses. One had always to be alert to where one stepped.

We had three household servants plus a part time gardener, and a *gardien de la nuit* or night watchman. The French had introduced social legislation into Africa. Servants' duties and hours were regulated, and we paid a social security tax. Since Louie, our cook/server was limited to a continuous eight-hour shift, he came at noon and worked through dinner. Christine, the nanny, came days when we were not going out and evenings when we were. Jean the laundry boy came in the morning. We never really got to know the gardener as he worked for a contractor and pretty much came and went as he pleased. Alphonse, the *gardien de la nuit,* came at dusk and left at first light.

Louie could do simple family meals and was a good server, but he was not a chef. Nancy prepared the dishes for guests. When we first arrived and before we hired Louie, Nancy was the full-time cook.

At her first prepared mean, David wanted to know where the fish course was. His mother explained to him he was no longer aboard a ship, and he would get all of his courses at once as long as she was the cook. When Louie joined us, we often had fish but it was not served as a separate course. This didn't upset David nearly as much as the order in which he was served. In the French manner, Louie served the ladies Madame first and Mademoiselle second. As *Le Patron* I was served third and as *le petit garcon* David was served last. He took it only so long, and then one night complained in no uncertain terms about being served last. In spite of Louie's disapproving look, I changed the order: Nancy, Suzy, David and then me. This seemed to satisfy David, but he still sniffed his disapproval when the fish came around as simply part of the main course.

Shortly after we arrived, the Ambassador invited Nancy and me to Sunday dinner. I told him we appreciated the invitation, but we tried to keep our Sundays free to be with the children since we tended to be so active socially during the week. The Ambassador was a little taken aback at this refusal. He thought a moment and then said "OK then bring the children!" UH! OH! We really didn't look forward to this. Suzy was five and David was four. Nancy sat them down and told them what to expect. She told them there would be lots of glasses and china and an array of knives and forks. David brightened when she told him the meal would probably be served in courses. She didn't worry about their table manners. She set a high standard there as a matter of course.

As it turned out we were the only guests. The kids were magnificent. Suzy sat on the Ambassador's right and totally charmed him. She served herself with aplomb as the waiter offered the courses, and she and the Ambassador carried on a cozy conversation. David on the Ambassador's wife's right was equally poised. He wowed the lady during the fish course by handily separating his fish from the bone with his knife and fork . She looked a little puzzled when he remarked to her how nice it was to have "real" fish.

The American Embassy in Cameroon like those in most other Third World countries during the Cold War was over staffed. We had the full panoply of attaches, military mission, AID mission, USIS library and so forth. There were probably thirty Americans in the Embassy plus local employees. As Economic Officer, I didn't really have much to do. As I mentioned earlier the main import into Cameroon from the United States was used clothing. These came in bundles, and were sold in markets throughout Cameroon. Once in an isolated part of the country I encountered a young man of college age wearing an Ohio State sweatshirt. When I hastened to greet him, he beamed a smile back displaying an impressive set of filed teeth, definitely not a "Buckeye."

Given the minimal level of US national interests in Cameroon, it would have been a good two-man post, an Ambassador and a young officer as his aide. To begin with the French effectively still ran the place. Mainly we just wanted to make sure Cameroon didn't slip into the Soviet orbit by default. So I fretted and looked for things to do. A high-level visitor from Washington counseled me to relax. "Learn another language; improve your tennis game; take up golf. This is what one has to do in these kinds of places." He told me "No one gives a damn about Africa anymore. If we could detach the continent from Asia at Egypt float it down to the Antarctic and sink it that would be just fine. Peter you have had two exceptional assignments to Ethiopia and Malaysia. You can't expect a string of these particularly in Africa." He said some nice things to me about my performance in Addis and Kuala Lumpur and my future prospects. "Peter you just have to be patient".

Well, at least he was honest, but it was a blow to hear this. Neither we nor the kids were happy with the school. Nancy had been doing her bit coaxing the kids to kindergarten everyday.. Now she was doing the same getting me off to the Embassy every morning. We had long conversations about our future. Nancy said she could teach the kids herself. "They might not learn French certainly not from me. But I can educate them. I am a teacher after all." Well that was one problem handled, sort of.

I felt trapped. I was a French-speaking Africanist. I had made this bed and I was going to have to lie in it. I liked being a Foreign Service officer. I liked most of the people I dealt with. We had interesting friends. We lived a quite comfortable life in most respects. I had been assured I had good prospects in the Foreign Service. Becoming an Ambassador some day was not out of the question. But on a day-to-day basis I simply didn't have enough to do, and this was something I was compulsive about. I could not stand being underemployed. I wasn't relaxed enough or emotionally prepared to find ways to occupy my time – learn a new language, play tennis or take up golf.

I did try. I went to Doula, the port, to see what was going on. Doula was the terminus of Pan Am's service from New York to West Africa.

The local manager told me he was doing OK on passenger traffic but freight was a problem. From the US out business was pretty good but the planes usually returned to New York empty. Later that afternoon I was talking to the Cameroonian owner of a local fishing company. His problem was the local market couldn't absorb all of his catch. "Do you catch shrimp?" I asked. "Tons," he said. I got him and the Pan Am manager together and felt good about a day's work for the first time in a long time.

I took some trips into the bush and met a local king. The king sat on a throne and we communicated through his chamberlain, a distinguished old gentleman who lay with his face on the dirt floor while translating my French into the king's local language and vice versa. As was the custom, I brought the king a very nice coffee thermos as a gift.. He was most appreciative as the one he had was broken. On my departure, he had the chamberlain give me a number of tribal artifacts. One of these was a bow with a quiver of poisoned arrows. The king's village of several thousand inhabitants was of particular interest because every building in it was constructed of earth bricks with tree-branch supports and thatch roofs. The road into the village some several miles long was covered with hand-woven, thatch, mats to keep it from becoming impassible during the rainy season.

I visited the missionaries in the area. One lived near the king's village. He took care of the king's trucks and was the person you saw to arrange an appointment. He was a mechanical genius and could fix anything. He ran his own lighting system off of a biomass gas plant. He had designed a bicycle-powered washing machine. His wife bottled her own root beer. One of his children had a monkey for a companion that pulled the baby's cart. He told me he hadn't had much success in converting any of the locals and his church would have recalled him were it not for his relationship with the king. He was a very happy man. He was clever and he felt needed. His wife seemed happy too. They recalled to me the phrase in The Book of Common Prayer "the peace that passeth all understanding." When I told her about the trip, Nancy said, "Maybe the wife was happy because her husband was happy." "OK, obviously I am not happy. Are you unhappy too?" She wiped away a tear. That did it.

The next day I told Nancy I was going to resign. She didn't object. "What are we going to do?" my biblical Ruth asked. "How would you like to go home to New Orleans?" I asked. Ruth smiled.

Chapter 7. New Orleans

I was fortunate that I had a place to land. My grandfather had founded a cargo surveying firm in New Orleans back in the early 1900s. Two of my uncles had succeeded my grandfather. I had worked for them during the summers when I was home from college. A.M Juge & Co. was a venerable, bulk cargo-surveying firm in the Port of New Orleans. As my Uncle Maurice had pointed out during an earlier visit to New Orleans none of the grandchildren seemed interested in joining the firm and carrying on the Juge name in the port. So when I wrote from Yaounde that I was ready to do just that Maurice's response was "Come on home."

There was a certain aspect of "the prodigal son" to our return. Our parents were relieved we were out of Africa. My brother said he never understood why I had left "paradise" to begin with. Some of my cousins were disappointed there wasn't a diplomat in the family any longer. Everyone was most warm and welcoming. We settled comfortably back into the breast of the family. The kids were happy in their school, not that they didn't complain about things from time to time. Once, David decided to run away from home. I don't remember now what set him off. While Suzy watched, he packed a suitcase with a few clothes, but mostly toys. As he headed for the front door Suzy tried to talk him out of it. Suzy pointed out, "What are you going to do for food? You are going to get very hungry, and you are going to be cold. It is very cold outside." Once outside, he slowed a bit, and then turned into our garage. "Why are you going there?" Suzy asked. "Well" David replied, "Mom won't have to go so far to bring me my food, and it should be warm enough in the garage."

There were some feelings of alienation at times too. On hearing an announcement over the school public address system that all foreign children should report to the office to pick up information for their parents about alien registration, David got out of his seat and headed for the office. When his teacher asked him where he was going David replied, "I'm an Ethiopian." Suzy sensed a feeling of distinctness too. She asked one time if we were going to ride on a float in a Mardi Gras parade because we were so "different." No doubt she'd heard this said about us by one of the relatives.

Nancy was happy being back close to her folks. She fell into the pattern of the American housewife, mother, cook, cleaner, chauffeur etc. etc. We both missed the social aspects of our life overseas, the cosmopolitan friends, the dinner parties, and the conversations we had. Nancy said she missed those things more even than she missed having servants.

A.M. Juge & Co. had provided a good living for my grandfather and after him for my uncles. My role was to fit into the way things had been done and in due course all would be mine. What is it about a man in his thirties that makes him chafe in such circumstances? The Port of New Orleans was in decline and losing traffic to Houston and even Gulfport. Thinking of the future I looked for ways to expand the firm's business. I came up with the idea of going into damaged cargo surveying. We handled a case involving a barge fire. I was able to determine there was lots of unaffected product still in the barge. I tried to convince my uncles to buy it at a distressed price and sell it at a profit. My uncles were not interested. I could understand their position. They were content with what they had and not really looking to risk money developing a new line of business. So I settled down into the routine, but I couldn't shake the urge for new things to do. Is there such a thing as a mid-thirties crisis?

I began to look around for a way back into the Foreign Service or some sort of challenging life overseas again. After some false starts the opportunity came along. Mobil Oil Corporation needed an Africanist in Nigeria where the company was making a major investment in bringing on an offshore shore oil field in the middle of a war. Biafra the former eastern region of Nigeria was fighting a battle to secede from the Federal Republic of Nigeria. The Biafrans had just introduced light bombers into the conflict and no one had any idea how long the war would last. Mobil's General Manager was an experienced petroleum engineer; but he had never been in Africa before. One of the senior Mobil executives in New York, who was a former Foreign Service officer, decided the man needed a government affairs advisor. Following interviews in New York, they offered me the job.

The reader may well wonder how I, who elected to withdraw from a foreign post where one of his main concerns was the welfare of his children, could even consider taking his family with him to a war zone? The best answer I can give is that I researched the situation to my satisfaction. I convinced Nancy that the Biafran war was not going to be a threat to us in Lagos, where we would live. There was a good American school for the kids. Africa was always Africa with its challenges that we knew well. We focused on the positive things that we missed and rationalized the negatives. Informing our parents was not an easy matter.

I wish I could remember their reactions when we presented this to Suzy and David. I do recall one of them asking if we would be near the rain forest where kola nuts come from. "Sure" "there is rain forest there." "Good! That's where Pepsi comes from," I was informed. This they had learned from a TV commercial.

Chapter 8. Mobil

When Nancy and I interviewed with Mobil, its corporate headquarters were located on 42nd Street in Manhattan. Mobil put us up at the Drake Hotel on Park Avenue. We had a great evening with a Mobil friend we'd known in Malaysia. It was he who had told me about the Mobil opportunity. The next morning, Nancy and I went through a round of interviews at Mobil. We met a gentleman who was the director of Human Resources for Mobil's International Division. He was a former Foreign Service officer, and it had been his idea to bring an FSO in to advise the Mobil General Manager (GM) in Nigeria. He described the GM as "a bull in a china cabinet who carries around his own china cabinet in case there isn't one handy." He was not only unfamiliar with Africa he was unfamiliar with Mobil, and dishes were crashing about him all over the place. I was told my job would be to help him stay out of trouble. It sounded like "mission impossible" to me. But as the day went on and we met a variety of Mobil executives with experience in Africa, the opinion seemed to coalesce that I was just the guy for the job.

I was invited back a couple of days later to meet the President of the Exploration and Producing Division of Mobil and the Corporate Vice President for Government Relations. I also had a session with the new

GM of Nigeria, the man who was the GM in question. He was big and brusque, but he appeared to be smart, and he listened. We hit it off. He liked the fact that I was also an outsider to Mobil. He had been brought in as GM for Nigeria from a top job at ARAMCO, the Arabian American Oil Company, of which Mobil was a part owner. He had a reputation for being tough, but able to get things done. He told me he wanted me to focus on learning Mobil. He was having more problems with the New York Headquarters people than with the Nigerians. I was made an offer, more money than I thought I'd ever earn, and they laid out a familiarization program with Mobil and the oil business that would last about a month.

WOW! Mobil didn't mess around! Here it was just three weeks from the day I'd heard about the job, and I was hired. It had been straight talk all the way. I liked that, and I was impressed with the caliber of the people I met. Nigeria was a very important exploration and production play for Mobil, and I was going to be right in the middle of it. If all this wasn't enough, the lady who explained how Mobil handled expenses put the cherry right on top. I had asked about allowances. "We don't have allowances. We pay all of your expenses whatever they are, as long as they are reasonable. This means we don't expect you to lose any money while you are on Mobil business,. but we don't expect you to make any money from expense reimbursements, either. It's a matter of trust. Your boss approves your expense claims and, he will know if you are trying to rip off Mobil." Then she paid me in *cash* for my expenses thus far. WOW! again. So I signed on and I never looked back.

When school was out, Nancy and the kids joined me in New York. Mobil moved us into a two-bedroom furnished apartment in Beekman Towers right across from the UN building. There was a nice park just behind it. The first time we visited the park we noticed there were no children but lots of dogs in spite of the sign on the gate that prohibited dogs. A kindly gentleman informed me that this was the dog park. "The children's park is just over there," he pointed. We were learning New York, too.

One weekend when heading over to Central Park, I called David up short for running too far ahead of us. "We could get separated," I said. "Then what would you do?" He thought a minute and said, "I'd hail, a taxi and have him take me to the Beekman Towers." Pretty good answer for an eight-year-old, I thought. Suzy said her plan if she was separated from us in Manhattan, was to hail a taxi, and tell him to take her to the Mobil Building where she would ask for Mr. Youngblood. He was the Mobil executive who was coordinating my orientation program. Suzy had met him, liked him, and was fascinated by his name.

While we were in Manhattan the Apollo moon landing took place. We woke Suzy and David in the middle of the night to watch Neil Armstrong step on the moon. They stared glassy-eyed at the TV screen, mumbled their thanks, and went back to bed, but, by gum, they saw it! Our visas came though for Nigeria and my orientation came to an end after many interesting experiences including helicopter trips out to some offshore oil production platforms. I visited Mobil's research labs. I went to Washington to talk to the State Department Nigerian desk officer and the like. Three years after we'd last been there, we were headed back to Africa.

A. Nigeria

Nigeria's principal political dynamic is that the former British colony is divided into three main tribal regions. Hausa and Fulani tribal groups dominate the north. The west is the land of the Yorubas, and the east is Ibo land. The British left the country in the hands of a multi-tribal civilian government in 1960. Mobil's GM had a hard time understanding the parliamentary system of government the Nigerians had inherited from the British. One of my jobs was to try to help him understand this. He was not a quick study. Instincts he had learned in the Kingdom of Saudi Arabia led him astray. For example, he found it hard to believe that the Permanent Secretary of the Petroleum Ministry was every bit as important for him to cultivate as the Minister of Petroleum. "Why, he's just a bureaucrat," the GM commented.

Inter-tribal rivalries and corruption marked the years after Nigeria's independence in 1960. Ibo-dominated military officers overthrew the Hausa-Fulani and Yoruba civilian rulers of Nigeria in 1966. There was a bloody reaction against the Ibos, and in 1967 they initiated a war of secession from Nigeria. The Ibos called their country Biafra after an ancient African kingdom of the same name. The war had been in progress for two years when my family and I arrived in August 1969. The oil fields discovered by Mobil in 1966 were offshore in Biafran waters. Mobil had abandoned their base headquarters in the east when fighting first broke out, and ultimately relocated to Lagos. The fighting was then concentrated in about the middle of the east region. The federal Nigerian forces appeared to have gained the upper hand at first, but then the Biafrans began to receive outside assistance in the form of some light bombers. They had recently carried out a bombing raid on a Shell Oil facility in a liberated zone on the coast inflicting considerable damage, and some fatalities.

Mobil was constructing an offshore production platform in the field. Drilling rigs were completing development wells and a specially outfitted tanker was scheduled to arrive in six months to begin functioning as a temporary production terminal. New York management was getting nervous. As soon as we arrived, the GM put me to work on a number of projects. One, he had me pull together a basic information book on the overall enterprise. He then designated me to compile and write a combined, weekly report to New York, "because you can write." I think it was more because he figured he could control my report. He wasn't sure about the Mobil guys who used to send their reports in separately.

He had me sit in on meetings where the GM "tried to figure out" New York's cables and compose his replies. There was no such thing as a phone call between New York and Lagos in those days. At the GM's meetings when matters got tense the GM was inclined to yell. Sometimes I yelled back. I thought this was the way people communicated in the oil industry, but I noticed the Mobil people simply clammed up when he started yelling.

After a short stay in a hotel, we moved into a house on Victoria Island. Nancy got the kids registered in school, hired servants and set about getting the house in shape. We had bath towels for curtains to begin with. The Nigerian American School was located, due to a quirk of history, in the middle of a Nigerian Army Base. Perfectly safe as long as we were all on the same side. The school had a tie-in to the Tacoma Washington public school system. Teachers were transferred back and forth from Lagos to Tacoma and the school was plugged into the same system for textbooks, curriculum development and the like. We were very happy with this school and so were the kids..

Because of wartime import restrictions, shopping was sort of like hunting. Sometimes Nancy returned with variety in her bag, sometimes not. Lagos was on the coast and there was plenty of fresh fish, so we ate well enough. There was a sense of community between the expatriates and Nigerians. We were all in the same boat, and we pulled together because of the war. We did encounter many military checkpoints as we traveled about Lagos and the countryside. These could be scary. One night, we were coming across the bridge from Lagos Island to Victoria Island when we were stopped. An obviously drunk soldier pointed his rifle in the car, and ordered the four of us out. Suzy asked, "What do they want?" I explained to her they were looking for guns. "Are they running out?" Suzy asked. The soldier had obviously found some whisky in a car during an earlier search, and was really looking for more whisky.

About early October, the GM told me he wanted a prediction of when the war would end. WHAT? He explained to me that Mobil operated on planning cycles. The affiliates went into New York in the fall with a set of business assumptions. Based on the assumptions, the planners in New York developed the affiliate's business objectives. He needed an assumption of when the war would end, so the planners could calculate when oil production would commence. Then they would set production objectives for the next five years. "You have three days for a date and supporting rationale."

Over the next two days, I talked to everyone I knew in Nigeria, the political and economic officers at the Embassy, the Military Attaché, British friends, Dutch friends, Austrian friends, our cook who was from the east, and a cross section of Nigerians.

The only Nigerian *friend* I could claim in the short time I was there was the Governor of the Eastern State. He was an Ibo, but as a matter of conscience he was one of the few Ibos who had sided with the Nigerians because he believed in the unity of Nigeria. We had been classmates in African Studies at UCLA. He told me he didn't envy me my task, and had nothing definite to offer, but he had his Ibo sources, and was probably even related to some of the Biafran leaders. He told me he didn't think the Biafrans could hold on much longer. He said the leaders were growing weary. This tracked with the Embassy political officer's view, but not the military attaché's. He thought the war would go on longer, maybe even to the end of the following year.

I let this run around in my head for a day, slept on it and then went into the GM's office. "Mid-February next year". (Three and a half months hence). "I can't give you a rationale for this. It's a judgment call based on what I know about this place and a lot of input. I can't blame anyone else for this. It's my call. I'm probably wrong." "No date certain huh?" the GM asked.. " Well, let's say February 15,1970." My knees knocked.

Later, after the assumptions report had reached New York, the GM told me he thought Mobil Management was getting cold feet. They had their sources, and they thought the war was not going to end anytime soon. They were becoming reluctant about risking the capital involved in bringing the tanker in to start production. They were concerned, too about the risk to Mobil people from a possible Biafran bomber attack. At this very time, the Biafran bombers attacked one of Mobil's marketing company's gasoline storage terminals. It was located about fifty miles from the fighting zone. The Mobil Nigerians who manned the terminal did a fantastic job fighting the resulting fire. No one was hurt and the damage was limited, but it scared the hell out of New York.

The Mobil Board summoned the GM to New York. He anticipated what this meant, and without a word to anyone, he secured an urgent appointment with Nigeria's head of state, General Gowon. Living up to his reputation as a bull in a china cabinet, flatout, he told the general he needed to know when the war was going to end. He said he needed this information for Mobil's top management in New York who were facing some difficult decisions about proceeding with substantial investment to begin oil production in Nigeria.

The general gave the GM a response in words to this effect: Generals may have some idea of when a war is going to begin but they seldom know just when one is going to end. It is up to Mobil's management to make the business decision about when they will commence oil production. Tell them Nigeria needs the revenue from Mobil's production badly, and after the war is over, Nigeria's leaders will remember who stood by them, and who didn't ,GULP!

The GM carried this message back to Mobil's top management. They didn't like hearing it, and some of them carved mental notches in their canes about this GM who had forced their hands with

his rash action of getting the Nigerian head of state involved. If Mobil wanted a long-term future in Nigeria, the corporate board was left with no option. It wisely decided to stay on plan.

In a wonder of damned fool luck for me, guess what! the Biafran leaders surrendered to Nigeria on February 15, 1970, ending the war. This was the very day in the assumption we had sent in to New York.. The GM picked the date, but it was based on my prediction of mid-February. The GM gave me the credit. On the same day, as a matter of complete coincidence, the converted tanker **Mobil Japan** dropped anchor off the coast of Nigeria. I became briefly famous in Mobil. I guess that was my 15 minutes.

The GM on the other hand, ended up with the enmity of Mobil's top management. He had forced their hand, and caused them discomfort *and* he had been right! The Nigerian Permanent Secretary of Petroleum who didn't like the GM to begin with, let it be known he thought Mobil had been holding the tanker off shore until the war ended. The GM's days were numbered. I thought maybe mine were too.

Shortly thereafter, we celebrated the first shipment of crude, and right on the heels of that, the GM was transferred. He was reassigned to ARAMCO. The new GM was a petroleum engineer who had grown up in Mobil. He was a veteran of two major Mobil exploration plays, Venezuela and Libya. He did not need a government relations adviser nor anyone to help him read Mobil management. All the old Mobil hands were ecstatic about his coming. The Human Resources Manager was due for another assignment after several years in Nigeria. Mobil offered me the job as his replacement. It was a substantial promotion. I told them I didn't know anything about human resources. Responding that they thought I could learn what I needed to, I was moved under the present HR Manager until he departed a couple of months later. The new GM told me Mobil had decided it could make a Mobil "hand" out of me. "And besides, people are not exactly lining up to come to Nigeria as the HR Manager."

So life with Mobil continued. We were happy it did. I began to learn Human Resources. This function in Mobil, particularly in one of its foreign affiliates covered a lot of ground. In addition to all the traditional personnel administration tasks of labor relations, compensation and benefits administration, recruiting, training, and career development, this function overseas also included public affairs and government relations. In Nigeria, Mobil put all of this under a Relations Manager with the Human Resources Manager reporting to him. The new Relations Manager also came to Nigeria from Libya.

After the war, we took trips into the bush. We visited a game park on the Niger River, a spring-fed swimming hole for picnics a couple of hours away, and several of the major Nigerian cities. Nigeria was the most populous country in Africa with some 50 million people.

When we were there. Nancy bought an African Grey parrot from a bird dealer. He spoke a blue streak, and must have formerly belonged to a British bachelor. His accent and vocabulary betrayed this. Every now and then he'd shake his head and say "Gawd! Fifty million of em!" You had to be careful what you said around parrots.

Nancy refereed the Friday afternoon softball game in our front yard. There must have been a dozen kids from the neighborhood who came by every week for this. Nancy got involved because she got tired of hearing the constant arguing about calls. She took over and the kids rarely challenged one of her calls. I was elected a member of the school board.

I had a GP-14 sailboat that I sailed in Lagos harbor. Much of the time David went with me. We belonged to the Lagos Yacht Club where there were a number of other GP-14s. Sailing the harbor could be tricky dealing with the strong currents, and the heavy freighter traffic coming and going. David and I were rammed by a steel-hulled workboat that had no look out posted, and no one at the wheel. Incredible but true. We saw the boat heading right for us, but couldn't maneuver out of the way because the wind and current were both against us.. We managed to line ourselves up so as to take the ramming bow-to-bow. My boat was swamped. David was thrown into the water one way, and I the other. Fortunately there were other boats nearby that picked us both up. We were none the worse for wear, but my boat required some work before I could sail again.

With Mobil one got to take home leave every year. We went with mostly empty suitcases as the kids had worn out or out grown all their clothes and there were no acceptable replacements locally. David's last pair of serviceable shoes were on his feet, and just barely holding together. We were all pretty threadbare. When we went through customs at JFK the customs inspector looked up from our bare suitcases, gave us the once over, and smiled "Missionaries?" he asked. I nodded. Nancy looked arrows at me. She made up for this later in the shops.

On our return to Nigeria from home leave we spent time in Europe and acquired a Yorkshire terrier puppy in London. The airline agents were equivocal about whether the puppy could go in the cabin with us on our flight to Lagos. "It will be up to the aircraft commander" they said. I don't think Suzy took a full breath until we finally heard that the puppy could go in the cabin with us. After we were airborne, Suzy penned a note to the aircraft commander thanking him for allowing "Raffles" in the cabin. A stewardess took the note forward and returned with an invitation for Suzy to the flight deck. While Suzy was up forward, the plane dipped its wings slightly to the left and then to the right. "Uh! Oh!" David exclaimed with concern "Suzy's driving the plane." She came back to her seat aglow with stories about the aircraft commander. It was nice to return to Lagos. This was home.

Within a few months of our return to Lagos however Mobil offered me a job in New York at Mobil's headquarters. This was a very good thing for me. It meant I was being accepted as a Mobil "hand" and the position offered was an interesting one. Strangely, following the end of the war Nigeria was quickly becoming a more dangerous place to be. With the Mobil oil field on stream and exports of oil from all the other fields unimpeded, the petro dollars had begun to flow into the country. Barriers to imports had been lifted and after the long austerity of the war years, Nigerians were spending like crazy. People left their farms in the country and flocked to Lagos and other cities where they expected to find the streets paved with gold. There were no jobs for these people as yet. Poverty and crime rose hand in hand. The police began publicly executing captured thieves by firing squads. We were not sorry to leave. We packed up everything and said our goodbyes to our friends. Off we went with our usual eighteen suitcases, a dog, and one African Grey parrot.

B. New York

Working for Mobil in New York for families with school-aged children in the 1970's meant living in the surrounding suburbs, and commuting to Manhattan by train. Our chosen suburb was Westport, Connecticut. While Nancy looked for a house, we stayed at the New Englander Motel. A maid opened the door one evening when we were out to dinner, and Raffles bolted. When we returned to the room, the parrot was very agitated. The maid had left a note of apology. We looked and called for him everywhere, but there was no sign of him. He was gone for three days. It snowed one day, and we were sure this little African dog was done for. He had never been cold a day in his life. Those were sad times. We advertised in the paper and on the radio.

Suzy and David could not believe their new school. There were frequent food fights in the cafeteria. At first when the other kids asked them where they were from, they answered Nigeria. They learned this was a mistake. They were looked at like they had just stepped off the moon. We were all brightened by Raffles' return. A lady who owned a kennel saw him hanging around the other dogs. She had seen our ad and called us. He was scruffy and hungry but otherwise OK. We treated him to his own cheeseburger that night. One day, Suzy asked us who her orthodontist was. This was apparently a Westport social litmus test. The other question was, what religion they were. David wanted to know if he could change from Episcopalian to Catholic. It was easier to say.

Nancy found a great house overlooking Long Island Sound. It was near to another school and the town-owned country club. The house belonged to the widow of a Mobil man who had served in India and China. It was just two blocks from the beach and two restaurants. We could barely afford it, but we stretched and moved in. The parrot introduced us to the neighborhood by shouting out the window, "Nixon's a fink!" It was the Watergate era and the parrot had picked up where we stood on the issue. I was standing at the window one day watching as new neighbors moved in next door. The parrot let go with a wolf whistle when the wife appeared in shorts. She swung around and saw me standing at the window. "What kind of creep do we have for a neighbor?" you could see written on her face. "It was the parrot," I yelled over to her. "Yeah yeah!" she yelled back.

The kids liked the new school much better than the first one. Someone seemed to be in control. As spring and summer arrived, they loved living by the water and the country club. They did everything there was to do including tennis and swimming lessons. We bought a catamaran and moored it in Compo Cove just down from our house. Nancy accommodated again to life without servants.

I liked my job at headquarters. I worked on manpower planning in the International Division. However, I hated the damned commuting. Monday to Friday was one long workday in Mobil. I took a six o'clock train in the morning, and returned after seven at night. But the weekends were great. I traveled to Mobil's overseas affiliates a lot. I was gone as much as a third of the time. Had this been our lifestyle from the time the kids were born, I don't think we would be the same family we are. I certainly wouldn't have the same relationship I have with them today.

Money was tight even though I made a very decent salary. Suburban New York living just seemed to gobble up every penny.

One vacation, I suggested camping for several days on Cockene Island on Long Island Sound as a cheap outing. We sailed over to the island on the Hobie Cat towing a skiff behind. The parrot and Raffles went with us. Nancy and Suzy left after the first night. They did not like being on an island that rats made home. The rats never actually approached us, but we heard them all night long scampering over a dump of abandoned beer cans not far from our campsite.

New York was a successful assignment for me. At the end of eighteen months I was offered the Relations Manager's job at Mobil's major new affiliate in Indonesia. Mobil had just concluded negotiations with the Indonesians to develop the Arun gas field on the Island of Sumatra. With thirteen billion cubic feet of recoverable natural gas, Arun was the largest producing gas field in the world at that time. A large portion of Mobil's total income was to come from this venture for a long time. The Arun field continues production today but the reservoir is approaching effective depletion. The company has had to shut down operations from time-to-time because of political turmoil in Aceh..

C. Indonesia

We flew out to Indonesia by way of Hawaii. We stayed at the old Moana Hotel on Waikiki beach and tried surfboarding. Nancy and I realized we were over the hill for this sport. Suzy and David took lessons and did quite well. Suzy was thirteen and becoming a young lady. One day she was carrying her board down the beach when she heard a voice calling "Hey Chick." She didn't think the voice could be referring to her. "Hey Chick" it came again. She turned. "Don't carry your board. Drag it like this;" the handsome young instructor came over to show her how. Oh my God I thought. She's already a chick. Suzy was charmed.

Mobil's base of operations was in Medan, a town on the Island of Sumatra. There also were offices in Singapore and Jakarta to handle various parts of the enterprise. We lived in Medan in a great house in the old Dutch residential area where mostly members of the Indonesian elite, and expatriates lived. The Arun field was located in the province of Aceh northwest of Medan, and a few miles in from the Straits of Malacca. In three hundred years of Dutch colonial rule, the Dutch never really controlled Aceh. The Acehnese fought the Dutch the entire time. When Indonesia won its independence from the Dutch after WWII, the Javanese recognizing the Acehnese' fierce attachment to their own independence, did not seek to impose the same strong central control from Jakarta that they did throughout the rest of Indonesia. We worked very closely with the Governor of Aceh in our operations there. We trained local Acehnese to take positions of responsibility in the enterprise rather than bringing in Javanese, which was what the central government wanted us to do.

This was the best job, and the most fun I ever had in Mobil. The General Manager was the best I'd ever seen. He was not only a superb manager of people, he thoroughly understood community and government relations and was a master at handling New York. He and I worked extremely well together. The Governor grew to trust us completely, and he pretty much kept Jakarta off our backs.

We instituted a training program for the sons of Achenese rice farmers and fishermen that was world class. It was the equivalent of two years at a technical high school. We selected the students by competitive exam. We hired a former Oxford professor who knew Indonesia well to run the program. He brought in British technical teachers and language instructors. The students had to know English to work with the American oil field hands from Texas and Louisiana. The basic sentences in English were very interesting coming out of the mouths of Brits—"Hey You! Get your ass over here." When the Louisiana and Texas supervisors arrived, they were amazed at how well the trainees understood English. The technical teachers taught basic math and physics and then moved the students on to hands-on gas field technology. We sent many of the trainees to colleges in the States. The first four graduated *cum laude* in petroleum engineering, two from the University of Texas, and two from the University of Oklahoma.

We fell into another extended family. Surtini, a Javanese woman of indeterminate age was the cook and majordomo. She loved Raffles. He essentially became her dog. Nancy let the house boy go soon after arriving when she realized Surtini didn't like him. She wanted a peaceful household, so she asked Surtini to hire his replacement. She brought in Nasri, a bright young Batak girl as the maid. I was assigned a car and driver. The driver was Udin. The gardener also named Udin was a gentle young man in his twenties with a large family to support. Under Nancy's experienced hand the house ran like a top.

Indonesia was a wonderful place to live. The country was beautiful. It was tropical rain forest with nearby mountains. The Indonesians were delightful, hospitable people. Indonesia has an ancient and fascinating culture. We traveled and enjoyed ourselves thoroughly. Mobil had a company plane that flew daily between Medan and Singapore. Employees and dependents were encouraged to use the plane on a space available basis, and there was almost always space.. Families went over to Singapore for weekends, and for medical treatment when needed. There were excellent hospitals in Singapore, and we had our own clinic and doctor in Medan.

Medan itself had a population of over a million people. It didn't feel that big because there were virtually no tall buildings, and the

Indonesian settlement pattern sort of merged into the forest. There was the Medan Club. The Japanese had used British prisoners to construct the club as an Officer's Tea House during the Japanese occupation in WWII. It offered tennis, movies and a restaurant. One of the European plantation companies opened their spring-fed swimming hole to families on weekends. In time we put in our own swimming pool.

Our garden was spectacular. There were over fifty different blooming plants including hedges of wild orchids. We had several tropical fruit trees including two varieties of mangoes. There was plenty of good food available in the markets that Nancy visited daily. In a local Chinese grocery good Scotch that had probably never been seen by a customs officer could be had for $5 a bottle. This was cheaper even than Singapore duty-free. Heineken brewed the local beer, Bintang. Mobil as well as all the consulates and trading companies maintained guesthouses in Brastagi, a mountain retrreat about an hour and a half from Medan. Mobil's guesthouse featured a huge fireplace and spectacular views of the mountains. There was a golf course at the former Dutch Hotel whose kitchen also served excellent nasi goreng, Indonesian fried rice. Further up into the mountains was Lake Toba, a huge fresh water lake formed by a volcanic explosion back in the mists of time. One evening, I came home from the office to find David and a buddy camping in our front garden. They had pitched a tent and were sitting in lawn chairs by the pool. Nasri was serving them lemonade from a tray. She then turned to tend the burgers she was cooking for them on a grill. "You call this camping?" I asked. "As you always say Dad, any damned fool can make himself uncomfortable."

As the development of the Arun field neared completion, the Indonesian Government required Mobil to move its headquarters from Medan to Jakarta the capitol of Indonesia. Production was scheduled to commence in mid-1977 and the Government's policy was to centralize the direction of all major economic activity in Jarkarta. So in December 1976 we moved from Medan to Jakarta. Surtini and Nasri moved with us. This was the first flight on an airplane for both of them. Nasri enjoyed the experience. She looked out the window, and had lunch, and talked with Suzy and David. Surtini never looked up from her lap. We moved into one of the grandest houses in which we have ever lived. Both Surtini and Nasri looked at me with heightened respect when they saw the place. An Indonesian general owned it. He built it to accommodate himself some day but in the meantime, he was happy to rent it to Mobil. Indonesian landlords were able to pay off their construction costs in about five years by renting such houses to Mobil and other international companies operating in Indonesia. It was white stucco with columns, had a circular drive up to the entrance and was surrounded by a lush garden. There was a central atrium with fishponds inside and out, marble floors and a large swimming pool in the rear garden. One of our neighbors told me later that when she asked Surtini who had moved in, Surtini replied, "an American general." We offered Suzy and David the option of staying in Singapore to avoid having to change schools yet another time. They didn't hesitate. "We're coming home" they said. They entered the Jakarta Joint Embassy School in mid-term. JES as it was called went through the 12th grade.

The Dutch ruled their colony of Netherlands East Indies from Batavia, the name the Dutch gave Jakarta, for over three hundred years. The Indonesians had an ancient culture and occupied the fourth largest country in the world in terms of population; In time they came to smart at the fact they were the colony of a minor European power. When the Japanese occupation of WW II ended, and the Dutch tried to reassume power, the Indonesians revolted. The battle for independence was bloody and protracted. There was a large Dutch military cemetery in Banda Aceh. The Acehenese tended the cemetery beautifully. The graves were kept up, flowers planted and whitewashed rocks outlined the paths. Occasional planeloads of Dutch relatives came to Banda Aceh to visit the cemetery. They wept when they saw the place. They couldn't believe their eyes at its beauty and the respect the Acehenese accorded it. It was not unusual to see elderly Dutch people and Acehenese crying and hugging one another.

There were still many of the Old Dutch colonial buildings in Jakarta. Canals the Dutch had built were still there, but were no longer flushed clean regularly with seawater. Mobil's corporate medical director came to Indonesia to evaluate local health systems, vectors of disease and the like. I took him to meet the Indonesian Minister of Health whose office overlooked one of these canals. As we were waiting for our appointment, I pointed out to him a typical Jakarta canal scene below. Upstream, an old man was squatting out over the water defecating. Fifty yards downstream some children were swimming. A few yards further down the canal a woman was washing dishes. "My God!" the medical director remarked, "I don't think we need to waste the Minister's time."

The island of Java swarms with people, perhaps one hundred million then. Jakarta was a large sprawling city, mainly houses with red tile roofs, but there was a growing high-rise city center. The first time I visited Jakarta in 1974, the old Hotel Indonesia that dated back to President Sukarno's time was all that there was. There were few large stores. Traditional markets prevailed. By 1977 there was a Hilton and several other modern hotels in downtown Jakarta. Traffic in the city was a nightmare. In addition to the usual cars busses and trucks there were thousands of bicyclists, pedestrians and betchaks (pedicabs) all going at different rates of speed. It took me up to forty-five minutes to reach the office by car. The kids rode almost an hour on the school bus each way. We missed Medan. Similar to Sumatra, there were mountains down the center of Java. At Puncack Pass about two hours from Jakarta by car, Mobil had a weekend cottage. The elevation there was almost three thousand feet, and it was cool and pleasant.

There were also many historic ruins to visit on the island. The ancient Buddhist monument at Borobudur was over 1100 years old. Sir Stamford Raffles, the founder of Singapore, discovered it in modern times during the brief period of British rule in the 19th century. Raffles was the British Governor of Indonesia. The Dutch began restoration of the monument in the early 1900s. Resting on a base some 400 feet square the shrine is constructed of black volcanic stone. There are eight tiers topped by a stupa that rises100 feet from the uppermost terrace. The walls are lined with carved panels of bas-relief sculptures illustrating the progress of Buddha toward enlightenment. Muslim and other invaders chopped the heads off most of the stone Buddhas that covered the monument.

The mystic island of Bali was just two hours away from Jakarta by air. The Dutch administered Bali differently than they did the rest of Indonesia. This was for different reasons than their special treatment of Aceh. The Acehnese fiercely fought the Dutch for three hundred years. The Balinese humiliated the Dutch by not fighting them. The Dutch actually had a peaceful trading relationship with the Balinese until almost 1900. Then they fabricated a provocation so they could invade Bali and take control. After some initial skirmishing, it became obvious to the Balinese the Dutch would overwhelm them. So they prayed at their Hindu shrines, donned white funeral garb, and with their leaders in front simply marched en mass onto the Dutch guns. When word of the slaughter reached Europe, Holland was harshly criticized by their neighbors. The Dutch never really got over this. They were mortified. They did take control of the island. but with the lightest hand of any of their colonial possessions.

We spent a New Year's holiday at a traditional Balinese hotel on Senur beach with another Mobil couple and their two children. It was one of the most charming places we have ever been. The hotel comprised a dozen Balinese cottages situated in a garden. Each cottage had a connecting outdoor shower with orchids climbing the walls. Gardeners placed Hindu offerings of a few small flowers and some grains of rice at the base of trees or on a stone along the paths between the cottages The dining room was open air and looked out over the garden and the ocean. All of our meals were Balinese food and delicious. We were there a week with children ranging from 6 to 13 years old, and we ate every meal at the hotel dining room.

On the second morning of our stay, I arrived at the dining room to find the only other person at the table so far to be the six-year-old son of our friends, the Wilsons. I wished him good morning and sat next to him. David "kechil" (little David, to distinguish him from David "besar" our 12-year-old David) informed me he had already ordered breakfast for everyone. He was very proud of the fact that he remembered what everyone had ordered the morning before. I watched with amazement as giggling Balinese waitresses brought out the breakfasts for all eight of us. There was one problem, David kechil and I were the only ones at the table. The Balinese found this hilarious. The headwaiter said to me, "Tidak apa apa Tuan." (Never mind Lord.) "We'll bring fresh breakfasts when the others come." David kechil smiled as he dug into his Balinese pancakes.

One day about five months after our move to Jakarta, Nancy had just hung the last curtains in the living room when the kids arrived home from school. Suzy announced that day had been a good one. She finally was feeling at home at the Jakarta school. David added his agreement. He was beginning to make friends and had prospects for the tennis team. I arrived home a short time later, and asked everyone to come into the living room. As they gathered, Surtini and Nasri, too I announced that Mobil had offered me a very good job back in New York. I was not prepared for the stunned silence from Nancy, Suzy, and David. I expected the moans and tears from Surtini and Nasri, but the stony silence from my family was unnerving. They later filled me in on their conversation just before my announcement. We left Indonesia for New York when the school term ended in June.

We took Raffles over to Singapore and put him in the kennel there to be shipped to Westport after we arrived home. We had planned our trip home around visits to some places in Asia we hadn't yet seen. At a stopover in Hong Kong on our way to Taiwan and Japan we ate at one of those floating restaurants in Aberdeen Harbor. The food was excellent but not the quantity we were used to getting in Indonesia and Singapore. So about halfway through the meal I beckoned the waiter over and ordered everything again. The kids applauded. The waiter smiled. They gave us postcards as well as fortune cookies with the check. We mailed one to Raffles at the kennel in Singapore. We found it in his kennel when he arrived at Kennedy Airport some weeks later.

We arrived at Honolulu at almost the same time as Nancy's parents who were joining us for a week on the island of Maui. They had waited until then to tell us our parrot had disappeared. He (she?) had stayed with them in Noxapater Mississippi while we were in Indonesia. They suspected he had been kidnaped. African Greys had become very popular and valuable in the States. I told them I suspected he had overheard them talking about our return and he'd run away so he didn't have to go back up north. Some years later we tumbled on to information that our parrot was seen performing in a parrot circus in Florida. There was no question that he was ours. He danced, whistled Colonel Bogie's march and said "Nixon's a fink!"

D. New York

The Exploration and Producing (E&P) Division had been reorganized. All of Mobil's E&P affiliates reported into one Divisional President. I was named as one of two Area Executives. We looked after Human Resource and Government relations matters in the 15 or so E&P affiliates. I traveled more that half the time. Once again I was commuting by early morning train into New York from Westport.

Both Suzy and David worked during the summers. Suzy was a hostess at the country club restaurant. David was a bus boy at Allen's Clam House a popular Westport restaurant. Suzy spent her money; David saved his. He saved enough in fact to purchase an expensive camera. I met him at Grand Central station in Manhattan one afternoon to go with him to a 57th Street Camera Shop. As he came down the platform I noticed he had a pronounced limp. A porter standing next to me told me he had seen that kind of limp many times. It came from mothers having kids put their money in a shoe as a safety precaution. The porter said it would be difficult to estimate how many Connecticut kids had been relieved of their money by thieves who had seen them limping about the streets of Manhattan.

We took the kids into New York for plays and we went to the opera once. Mobil had a box at Lincoln Center that was available to the troops when the chairman wasn't using it. I don't recall the name of the opera, but we all agreed to leave "at the half" as David put it. The music was totally unmemorable and the soprano was so rotund that the little tenor's embraces didn't quite reach around her.

The drug scene in Westport was bad. Suzy's friends tended to be stars, the kids with good grades and the leaders, but as many as half of them smoked pot. Suzy told Nancy that at a party on the beach one evening, a guy tried to get her to try a puff. She declined. He continued to insist until another friend also a user backed him off, and said to the group "Look no peer pressure on Suzy. She has as much right not to do drugs as we have to do them." Tortured logic but it worked.

In the summer between Suzy's junior and senior year, she organized a two-week trip of visits to colleges for herself and David. Both of them had decided they wanted to go south to college. The visits started at the University of Richmond, and we made the rounds of some fourteen schools ending with Tulane in New Orleans. Suzy's early favorite was Sweetbriar in Virginia. She liked its studio art and art history programs, and the girls who showed her around really put the rush on. David liked Sewanee, the University of the South. He liked the faculty and students he met. They seemed to really want him to come there. Many of the admissions people at other schools did seem to behave at times like they were doing the kids a favor even talking to them. Neither Suzy nor David were SAT superstars, but their scores were good enough to get into the places they were looking at.

Later in the fall, Suzy visited Sweetbriar when it was in session. She called after one day there. Yes, the art program was great, but she didn't like the women's college scene. Most of the girls spent the weekends on the road driving to one or the other men's or coed schools. She wanted to go see Sewanee again. Sewanee was one of the tougher schools to get in, and I didn't want Suzy to be disappointed again. I telephoned the admissions director at Sewanee. I told him what had happened, and asked him for a reading on her chances of getting in before we sent her to Sewanee to have another look. The gentleman said he understood my concern. After a few minutes he came back on the line. He had reviewed her file. "Send her on down. We'll be happy to see her." "Suzy," I said. "You've got it made."

Nancy went with Suzy and hung out at the Sewanee Inn while Suzy stayed at a dorm with some of the students and made the rounds. As time passed, Nancy said Suzy began to glow. When they left the campus for the airport, a male students wearing a jacket and tie, and the academic gown that marked him as a member of the honored Order of Gownsmen carried her bag from the dorm to the taxi. He held the door open for her. "That did it," Suzy said. "Sewanee it is."

Other than the traveling demands my job was great. In time, I gained the trust of the E&P President and the GM's in the affiliates. I was able to carry delicate messages back and forth and my advice was accepted as "neutral." I was viewed as a non-threatening facilitator, and problem solver. I knew I was doing OK because the GM's were always happy to see me and I could get in to see the Division President almost at will. My principal affiliates were North Sea (UK), Norway, Germany, Libya, Nigeria, Houston, Colorado, and New Orleans.

I was in this job over 3 years. They were fascinating years with lots of job satisfaction. Since it had been a three grade promotion money had not been a problem this time. But the story I want to tell about this assignment has nothing to do with any of this. It has to do with the global reach of an international corporation like Mobil.

One fall Saturday afternoon I was raking leaves, when Nancy called to me, "Alex Massad is on the phone." Massad was the President of Mobil's E& P Division. He had made *Forbes'* Ten Toughest Managers list that year.

"I've got a job for you. The daughter of a U.S.Congressman who is a Mobil friend is traveling in Europe with a school group. She's in St. Petersburg now and the congressman received a phone call that she has fallen ill. She's on her way today to Helsinki. The congressman called the State Department. They said they would try to help but he was not confident they would move fast enough. Could Mobil help? I told him yes."

"Can you handle it Peter?"

"Yes Sir; I'll get right on it."

"Call the congressman directly to tell him how it's going. I'm going to be away for a few days."

So I got out Mobil's world-wide telephone directory. I telephoned the GM of Mobil Finland. I didn't know this man and he didn't know me .Alex Massad was not the head of his division, but he knew who Alex Massad was. It was Saturday evening in Helsinki. The gentleman was hosting a dinner party. I explained the problem, and asked if he could help. "Absolutely. I'll get our physician to go see her at her hotel this evening."

The next morning I received a call from the GM in Helsinki. The doctor had seen the young lady the night before. She was suffering from traveler's diarrhea. He gave her some medicine and reported she should be OK in a day or two. I thanked the GM and rang off. I called the congressman and told him what had taken place in Helsinki.

Her next stop was Stockholm. So I got out the directory again and went through the same drill with the GM of Mobil Sweden with the same result. Next it was Oslo, and then Copenhagen. Alex Massad had returned, and called to tell me the congressman's daughter had asked her father to call off the Mobil doctors.She was feeling fine, and was embarrassed by all the attention. Besides, her classmates were beginning to wonder what was really wrong with her.

I wrote letters of appreciation for Alex Massad's signature to all the GM's. These people reported up through the International Marketing and Refining Division. So I then had to go apologize to my counterpart in that division for dealing directly with his GM's. He graciously accepted my apology. "It was probably the right thing to do under the circumstances," he said. I think actually he was just as glad he did not have to deal with Alex Massad.

E. Saudi Arabia

Saudi Arabia was our last overseas assignment. Suzy and David were both at Sewanee and were only in the country for visits during school vacations. Nancy and I were there for three years. It was not our favorite place.

I was an Arabian American Oil Company (ARAMCO) vice president. ARAMCO was founded by Standard of California, and joined over time by Texaco, Exxon, and Mobil. This was because there was more oil in Saudi Arabia than any one major oil company could handle. Saudi Arabia has one quarter of the world's proven oil reserves. In the decade before we arrived, the Saudis began buying out the interests of the four US companies in ARAMCO. They maintained the corporate shell as a matter of political convenience. The Saudis did not want to stir up ambitions among the various factions in the country over who would control the successor company to ARAMCO. A sort of shadow ARAMCO of the former US owner companies, called STEMCO (for Standard of California, Texaco, Exxon and Mobil) was set up within ARAMCO to represent the residual interests of the four companies. All the US companies still lifted considerable amounts of crude oil from ARAMCO. I represented Mobil in this group.

Nancy and I lived in Al Khobar where STEMCO occupied offices and apartments in a modern high-rise building. We had a penthouse apartment on the 14th floor of this building overlooking the Arabian Gulf. This is what the Saudis call the Persian Gulf. We could even see Bahrain from our apartment on a clear day. I had a car and a driver. I had a sailboat..There was golf and tennis in the ARAMCO compound. We made a number of good friends while there, but it was far from our favorite place.

I didn't have enough work to keep me busy. It reminded me of Cameroon. Nancy detested the place. She (and Suzy when she visited) had to wear dresses with high collars long sleeves and skirts down to the ground when in public, her "Mother Hubbard" she called it. The treatment of women in Saudi Arabia does not need expounding here. Nancy only stayed in the country to keep me company. Individual Saudis whom we came to know as friends were among the most gentle, kind people we have ever met, but the man in the street was a pig. They took great delight in groping foreign women in markets and shops. Once on a trip to a busy fish market, Nancy complained about several incidences of groping. Earlier, I had seen a fellow selling tools. I bought Nancy a small ball pin hammer that she kept in the folds of her dress and wielded with great effectiveness. I heard several yelps of pain as we made our way down a crowded aisle.

The country was full of single men of many nationalities who were there to perform the work the Saudis wouldn't do. Suzy said she used to feel like a piece of meat being observed by a pack of starving wolves when she went shopping with her mother. She spent no more time in the country than she had to. David spent more time. He had summer jobs there and enjoyed the novelty of going on dates chauffeured by my driver. Women were not allowed to drive in Saudi Arabia. We had a parking garage in the basement of our building. Just for the hell of it, Nancy used to take over from the drivers upon entering the garage. She would drive around the basement with élan to the great amusement of our Saudi drivers. Custom also called for women always to be escorted by men when in public. The ladies shopped in groups with a driver along as the required male escort.

Alcohol was strictly illegal, but was certainly available. ARAMCON's who lived in the compound made it in stills. I made drinkable red wine in our apartment. Great quantities of grape juice from all over the world, sacks of sugar, and cartons of baker's yeast covered the shelves of the supermarkets. It was an activity by foreign infidels the Saudi authorities turned a blind eye to as long as Saudi citizens were not involved. Going to church services was another illicit activity winked at by the government. ARAMCO brought in a Catholic priest, an Episcopal minister and two other Protestant ministers designated as teachers. They led services in gyms and other windowless buildings.

Islam weighed heavily on the common man in Saudi Arabia. The upper classes could fly to Europe for a break. There was seriousness to almost everything. You didn't hear a lot of spontaneous laughter. I was complaining about this one evening to some friends who had lived for a long time in Arabia. "Surely this is better than Nigeria," they said. It was a Saturday night. "No it isn't better," I replied. "Lagos on a Saturday night pulsated with people everywhere having a good time. There is just no joy here." There is beauty in the country. The dessert at sunset can be breathtaking. A drink from an oasis spring is especially refreshing. A market in an oasis can be a delight. A young sheep cooked by Arab friends with rice and vegetables, and served traditional style on a great platter while everyone sits around it on a carpet can be a real treat.

As a vice president, I was permitted to take Nancy with me when I left Saudi Arabia on business trips. I went on two or three of these a year. Nancy usually flew with me as far as New York and then headed on down to Sewanee to be with the kids. I went on to San Francisco, Houston, Westchester, Manhattan, and then met up with her in Sewanee to see the kids. Then we returned to Saudi Arabia after a week or so. On one occasion however she decided she wanted to accompany me. We used to have a saying in Mobil that "traveling with your wife on business is dangerous to your health." The ladies went along expecting naturally to have a good time. For the traveling executive, it was anything but, Trying to do both his job, and be a pleasant traveling companion to his vacationing wife could be stressful.

Anyway I welcomed Nancy along, but I warned her that it was not a pleasure trip for me and I might exhibit some strange coping behavior. She gave me a puzzled look, but shrugged as if to say, "Just what kind of strange behavior of yours haven't I already seen many times?" STEMCO vice presidents and their wives flew first class on business trips. Before the wheels were even up on take off, the Pan Am flight attendant brought me a double martini and Nancy a double scotch. Pam Am knew their First Class passengers on departing flights out of Saudi Arabia well. Nancy had dinner and watched the movie. After my third martini I stretched out and slept all the way to New York.

Fourteen hours later at JFK we connected with a flight to San Francisco. On arriving at the Hyatt Union Square Hotel after some twenty hours of flying, I was getting my second wind. Nancy was exhausted, but she was a trooper. She waited while I went off and had a massage, and then joined me for cocktails and a great dinner overlooking San Francisco Bay. She was quite happy to fall into bed at 9 PM. At about 1 AM I sat up in bed wide-awake. I turned on the lights and began to run a bath. "What are you doing?" Nancy moaned. "This is what I do," I answered "I have a meeting in the morning. I have to look over some stuff after my bath. Then I'll have a few hours sleep afterwards." She groaned and buried her head under the covers. So it went. I worked during the day; attending some tense meetings occasionally. These were not friendly visits to headquarters. Nancy shopped and went sightseeing. We had late evenings attending company dinners. I went through my routine at night; Nancy got very little sleep.

The trip ended in New York at the end of a week. By the time we were ready to head back to Saudi Arabia, Nancy was on her knees. I was feeling good about the results of my trip. It had been a business success, and I was feeling like celebrating a little bit on the Pan Am flight. Nancy fell asleep soon after takeoff and a couple of scotches, and slept all the way to Dhahran. I had champagne, caviar, dinner and conversation with a gorgeous Swedish flight attendant named Olu. She could see I was on a short leash with Nancy asleep next to me. So she was more attentive than might ordinarily have been the case. I learned Olu had never been to the gold market on her layovers in Dhahran. She had to have a male escort, and she told me all the pilots did was sleep on the layovers. I volunteered to take her. Once she established Nancy would be coming as well, she accepted, and asked to bring along her Danish friend, another flight attendant.

When we picked them up at their hotel the next evening, they were knockouts. Both were blondes. They had been to the beauty shop, were beautifully coiffed, and dressed in tight white slacks. WOW! I knew I was in jeopardy of being arrested by the Saudi religious police for bringing such creatures into a public place. I told Nancy who was in her Mother Hubbard outfit, "Look I'll stick close to Olu, and you stick close to Ola," Olu's only minimally less spectacular friend. Nancy replied, "No I'll stick close to Olu and Ola.. You lead the way." Fortunately there were no religious police about that evening, It was a good thing. One Saudi man, not paying attention to where he was going as he gawked at Olu and Ola walked straight into a lamppost. He staggered away holding his head. The girls got some amazingly low prices from the Saudi gold merchants for the items they purchased. Later at a restaurant in Al Khobar, we were treated to some of the most attentive service from the waiters I have ever experienced

I think I can fairly succinctly sum up what Saudi Arabia meant to us. Saudi Arabia paid the bills. We were there three years, and I covered all the kids' college expenses out of current income. And we had some great holidays together. One Christmas, I booked us into a suite at the Dolder Grand Hotel in Zurich. Our sitting room overlooked Lake

Zurich. We lived like royalty for a week. Another Christmas, Nancy and I flew to Sewanee. We then flew to Tokyo with the kids spending the New Year's holiday there at the Okura Hotel. Then we went to Singapore and stayed at the Shangri La Hotel for several days, and saw old friends from our days in Indonesia.. Suzy and David came back with us to Saudi Arabia for a few days, and then returned to school. We had gone right around the world on this vacation. On our last Christmas holiday from Arabia we took a Caribbean cruise. There wasn't much we missed doing, not bad compensation for living in Saudi Arabia.

In 1984 Mobil, Exxon, Texaco, and Chevron decided STEMCO wasn't working. It had not been successful in establishing itself as effective in representing the four companies vis a vis ARAMCO. Saudis preferred dealing directly with contacts in the companies rather through STEMCO. We shut down and left. We returned to New York. I was appointed to the position of International Human Resources Manager a senior position with lots to do. I was succeeding some 15 years later the man who brought me into Mobil in the first place.

F. New York

Once again the global reach of an international corporation like Mobil is demonstrated in my new assignment. Mobil had operations on every continent. There were over sixty Mobil marketing affiliates world-wide.

When I took over management of the group, not one of the 100 employees had a computer. I got one for myself and brow beat my secretary into getting one. Mobil had commenced down sizing to seek reductions in overhead. I winnowed my group down from a hundred to thirty-five in two years. Laying people off was tough. Fortunately the Mobil separation package was generous and most of the people did alright. When I left three years later, every employee had a computer on his desk. We were a third our former size, but at least two or three times more efficient.

I reported to the President of Mobil Marketing and Refining. My organization occupyied an entire floor of the Mobil building on 42nd street. I traveled a lot. Of the affiliates I visited, Mobil South Africa was one of the most interesting. Apartheid was still in full force. US companies with operations there were under pressure in the States to leave.

Mobil Oil South Africa had nothing to apologize for. It was one of Mobil's best affiliates and was way ahead of the curve in race relations. In fact, there were more black managers in Mobil South Africa per capita than there were in Mobil in the US. A black American Minister, Leon Sullivan created principles that US companies in South Africa were to be measured by. Mobil always ranked at the top. But eventually Mobil was forced to sell the company to a South African company. I think our Chairman grew tired of the public relations burden the South African affiliate posed.

I moved on to Mobil's Research and Development Corporation as Vice President for Human Resources. MRDC unlike other oil companies, concentrated all research and construction engineering in one organization. The others split the labs up among the operating divisions. Mobil had more patents than any other oil company.

It was a pleasant place to work. My office was in Princeton, New Jersey in a campus-like setting where basic research went on. The scientists were happy in what they did. I was able to help in a number of ways to foster their content. I made it possible for them to run experiments from home by computer where feasible. This permitted the fathers to do some baby sitting while their wives worked. I was then approached to make it possible for them and their wives to share a job; i.e. one would work 20 hours, and switch off to the other who would work 20 hours on the same project. I had to go to New York for approval with this one, and was shot down. Both people would earn benefits that cost about 25 % of salary. One fellow moved from one lab to another at a distance of less than 50 miles. He was turned down by New York for reimbursement of moving expenses. This guy had a hundred patents to his credit. I managed to have him reimbursed.

I traveled to the other labs in Paulsboro, New Jersey and Dallas. Once I had to replace a woman Human Resource Manager at one of the labs for not measuring up to the job. Her management had recognized the problem, but avoided taking action for over a year because of the possible repercussions. My days in New York had inured me from concerns for repercussions from firing people.

My bipolar disorder began to plague me again, and when my boss whispered in my ear that we were headed for downsizing in the labs, I decided I wasn't going to go through that again. I retired. I was 57 years old.

Chapter 9. Retirement

This has been one of my happiest times. I have time to do what I want, and virtually no deadlines. I attend damned few meetings, and I do not serve on any committees. I am in control of my life. I do pretty much what I want to do. I do pay attention to what my daughter and son have to advise, but seldom to anyone else.

I never dreamed being a grandfather could be so rewarding. I spend time with my grandkids. We have conversations. We exchange email. We tell one another jokes, some my daughter doesn't approve of. And how about this, they and their friends think I'm cool

I've had enough money. Mobil's retirement plan and my own 401K savings provided me with a good nest egg. I put this in the hands of a great financial manager at Burke & Herbert Bank, the oldest bank in Virginia. Through thick and thin, 16 years later my nest egg has shrunk, but I've got enough, and I've lived as well as I ever have.

Nancy and I bought a townhouse in Old Town, Alexandria. This was the fulfillment of a dream. All our married life we lived either in US Government housing, Mobil housing, or in the suburbs. Now we lived in a city within walking distance of restaurants, theater, and shopping. We later moved to another town house not far away that was on the Potomac River with a dock. I bought a boat.

I rent summer beach houses and fill them my daughter's and son's families plus the grandkids' friends. We toured Alsace a couple of years ago. We were on the QE2 on its last Atlantic crossing. We went to Ireland last June. I pay for all kinds of lessons. In Nancy's memory, who took great delight in shopping for clothes for Kate and Jack, I foot the bill for same, but no shopping for me thanks.

Kate and I had lunch after I picked her up from school one day when there was an early dismissal. We had a nice lunch together and talked about a lot of things. She is charming. It struck me that this 15 year-old who was good looking, trim, a straight A student who was active in things, suffered from low self esteem. I got her to talk about the "popular" kids at school. Why they were popular was complex, but one element stood out. Most of them had their own cars. So, I thought, I can take care of that. I bought Kate and Jack a car, an orange Honda Element. It's the coolest car at their high school.

Once, when the grandkids were younger I built a cabin in the West Virginia mountains. It was on twelve wooded acres in a valley. I put in a wood-fired hot tub. We went there every weekend until the kids entered middle school and high school, and were busy weekends. I went there by myself often with my dog. I wrote my first book there. This was the place where I broke my neck.

The dream faltered, Nancy died from metastasized breast cancer. She was 65. Her loss was a blow. Then came my turn. I suffered a series of heart attacks. The doctors brought me through that. Then came some lung problems. I could go on naming stuff, but this is the way it goes for old people. I'm now 74 with oxygen 24 hours a day, and an on-board pacemaker and defribulator. Everything is pretty much under control, and as Woody Allen put it, "I'm not afraid of dying I just don't want to be there when it happens."

During my hospitalization for the heart attacks, Suzy was driving 70 miles through rush hour traffic each evening to come see me. I recognized I had to move closer to her. So I moved from Old Town to the "independent living" part of a retirement community in Loudoun County, Virginia and then four years later, on to its "assisted living" unit. I am 10 minutes from Suzy and grandkids. "Falcons Landing" was founded by the Air Force Retired Officers' Community (AFROC). Most of the residents are retired military, but there are a few former Foreign Service officers and others.

Nancy found the place. She checked out several others and picked this one. It has lots going for it. One, I could bring my dog with me, two, there is a bar. We were going to move here together, but that didn't work out. Now at cocktail time, I invoke her presence when I open the soda for the scotch. It always spurts everywhere. Nancy used to fuss at me when I didn't hold the bottle over the sink. Now I always make sure I don't hold the bottle over the sink, then when it sprays all over, I pour and say, "Hello Nancy where in the hell have you been?"

I have volunteered in homeless shelters, and with meals-on- wheels, but mainly I have occupied myself by writing. My first book was about Suzy and David. Friends have often asked, "what did you do? How come your kids turned out so well? Was it living abroad?" I explored those questions in "Come Taste the Wine," I researched what educationalists call the "Third Culture Kid" phenomenon. Suzy and David certainly fit the definition, and I demonstrated this..

I couldn't interest a publisher or literary agent in the book. "No one is going to buy a memoir by a non-celebrity," I was told. There was no interest in the "Third Culture Kid" peg. So I went the Print on Demand (POD) route. I have published four books with Xlibris. In addition to "Come Taste the Wine," I wrote about my travels with Matey in France, and two books about Matey's adventures as an undercover CIA agent. Matey, by the way, is my dog.

I write the Matey books for my grandchildren. It would be nice if they sold, but they don't. I also published a collection of poems. I wrote some of them, dreadful stuff, but I had fun writing them. I am in the midst of writing another Agent Matey book now. One of these days I am going to tackle a novel about Paul Juge who commanded the European Brigade in New Orleans during the civil war, and was instrumental in surrendering the city to the Yankees.

Until recently, I used to go to France every year. I sometimes went twice, in April and September. I have stayed as long as a month, but most often for two weeks. I speak French. I stay in the 14th arrondisement in the south of Paris. It is almost totally residential with some wonderful restaurants. Often, I took Matey with me, but as he got older, he suffered spending so long a time in the cargo hold. The last time he went with me the flight was delayed, and Matey was some10 hours in his kennel on the plane. Once we were out of the terminal, and I could let him out of the kennel, he made a small lake. Then he looked me straight in the eye, and very effectively communicated, "Look, I'm not going to do this again. If you can't get me a seat in the cabin, then the hell with it."

I stay at the same small hotel on the Avenue Rene Coty. Over the years the manager of the hotel and I have become good friends. We always have drinks together. I take him to my favorite restaurant, and he takes me to his. An old school buddy lives several blocks from the hotel. He and I were fraternity brothers at LSU. I think he may know more people, and remember their names, than anyone else on earth.

He is a retired University of Paris professor. He has lived in Paris since 1968. He has written about twenty books, and has become famous for his Sunday evening salon. Some eighty or so people attend each week. It's a great place to meet people. Most of them are passing through, although there are a few regulars. Both French and English are spoken as well as a variety of other languages. There are always several people staying at his atelier, mostly girls.

Unlike most Americans, I find the French extremely hospitable. I have never encountered a rude Frenchman. I have a French friend from my Mobil days whom I always see when I visit Paris. A kinder person I have never met anywhere. I was in Paris just after US troops went into Iraq. There were anti-American demonstrations in the streets everyday, but when I asked Frenchmen who the demonstrators were, they shrugged and said Arabs and communists. The man on the street seemed to care less about Iraq. He was interested in soccer, bicycle and car races. This was reflected in the TV news programs. The French are becoming worried about the sizeable Arab minority in their country. There are roughly 5 million out of fifty million. The same percentage in the US would be 20 plus million.

The last time I went to Paris, I took along my handicap scooter. It comes apart and was easy to get on the airplane. What a difference it made. I can walk, but not very far. I become short of breath. Before, walking to my friend's house and my favorite restaurants was slow going; it meant several rest stops along the way to catch my breath. On my scooter, I zipped everywhere in a matter of minutes. These scooters have not reached Paris yet, and people stopped me on the street to find out where I got mine. The Police didn't know what to make of it. They would look at me then shrug. I stayed on the side walks. Apparently there were no rules to guide "les flics."

I often see my daughter, and son and their families. My son lives in Greenwich, Connecticut. I take AMTRAC up to see them from time to time. Last May we spent a week together in Kiawah. I have a beard, and my 4 year old granddaughter is not quite sure what to make of me yet.

My daughter has been incredible about looking after me. I don't think I could make it without her. She has arranged her work week to have Fridays off so she can take me to doctors' appointments and such. We do a lot together. I am at her house almost every weekend. Her husband is a good guy. He deserves a lot of credit. He puts up with me. My granddaughter, Kate is just starting her freshman year of college. She left the car behind for Jack, my 16 year old grandson. Jack, is special. He is a very good trumpet player, and an accomplished archer. How he is going to put these two skills together is a real puzzle, but if anyone can pull it off, he will. The car is his when he gets his license later this month.

I keep in touch with my friends: from college, from the Coast Guard, from the Foreign Service, and from Mobil. Thank God for email.

I see a lot of doctors, cardiologists, pulmanologists, internists, neurologists, and psychiatrists, to name just the regulars. I don't readily accept the tag of "functional alcoholic" that one of them pinned on me. Alcohol has not been a controlling factor in my life. I'm not an alcoholic. I just drink like someone from New Orleans.

I recently took a longevity test with questions about my lifestyle which was supposed to tell me how much longer I will live. I answered the questions honestly. My score has me living to 81. I am 74. Now, if that happens I will be the first octogenarian in my family in several generations.

In the meantime, I don't intend to change a damned thing.

To end, I quote this from my poetry book.

> "Life is not a journey to the
> grave with the intention
> of arriving safely in a
> pretty and well-preserved
> body, but rather to skid in
> broadside, thoroughly used
> up, totally worn out, and
> Loudly Proclaiming, WOW!!
> What a ride."
> Anon.
> (received on the internet).

Printed in the United States
111916LV00004B/207/A